GO

GOING HOME

A practical and pastoral
journey through bereavement

Michael Cole

Highland Books
Guildford, Surrey

Copyright © Michael Cole 1993

British Library Cataloguing-in-Publication Data. A catalogue record for this book is available from the British Library.

All Scripture quotations, unless otherwise noted, are taken from the *Holy Bible, New International Version*. Copyright © 1973, 1978, 1984 by the International Bible Society. Used by permission of Hodder & Stoughton.

Published by Highland Books, an imprint of Inter Publishing Service (IPS) Ltd, 59 Woodbridge Road, Guildford, Surrey GU1 4RF.

Printed in the UK by HarperCollins Manufacturing, Glasgow. Typeset by The Electronic Book Factory, Cowdenbeath, Fife.

ISBN No: 0 946616 96 5

Contents

Foreword

'**G**oing home' are two words that evoke different feelings in different people. We are glad to be going home from hospital. Anxious to be going home to an empty house at night. Lonely and sometimes devastated, to be going home after a funeral. Happy to be 'going home' to heaven as a Christian at the end of a long life. So this little book will provoke different feelings because it is written with at least three groups of people in mind.

Clearly, there will be many who have faced – or who are facing – bereavement. The second group consists of those who are faced with the prospect of caring for ill or elderly relatives, or are willing to face the question of their own illness and death. This group may also comprise those who care for the bereaved professionally.

Finally, there will be many others whose main concern is not illness or death, but the future. You have questions about whether there is a life after this one. What about heaven and eternity? Many issues arise in your mind.

Of course all these matters – personal, practical and pastoral, are closely linked together. They are stages along the road of life and death. It is a road that all of us have to travel, but none of us choose to do so. I am aware that we start out on that journey at different points and thus you may find it helpful to start at the point (chapter) that best fits your need.

It seemed best to take the journey in a logical order, so I have focused upon illness and death in chapters 2 and 3, and upon bereavement in chapters 4–6. I have written a special chapter relating to children because they also travel this same way with us (chapter 7). The future after death and the reality of heaven is our focus in chapters 8 and 9, while the possibility of making a new start, and building our lives again is the hope with which the book ends at chapter 10.

We have to start somewhere, so in chapter 1, I have tried to give some understanding of what death is, and the fact that other people have been asking exactly the same questions that are in your mind.

Perhaps I should say something about myself before going any further. Why am I writing this book? What experience do I have to write about death and bereavement?

There are many helpful books on various aspects of death and dying. I have read a number of them, and without fail I have been helped by them. However, I do not know any book that covers this whole range of practical, pastoral and personal questions that I have tried to answer for the man or woman who is taking the journey through bereavement. In my ministry I find the need for such a book, and so I have attempted to write it.

There have been occasions when I have drawn back from the task because I realise that I am dealing with the most painful and awful event in all our lives. Death is the one great certainty for everyone. This generation seems to have conspired not to speak about it, and thus we are, by and large, unprepared for death.

I can still feel the shock of the sudden and unexpected news of my father's death from a heart attack outside our back door. The memory of my mother's lingering death from cancer of the colon, which lasted about three years, is still very real. I have walked through that dark and lonely valley of death when our first son didn't live. I am aware that other people's glib answers don't help. I am aware that death will come to all. Yet, when it comes to a member of my family or someone close to me, it is I who hurt and need help and comfort. I have also visited, cared for and, I hope, helped hundreds of families at the time of death in my parish ministry, and as I get older I find myself privileged to enter into the very intimate feelings and pain of those who are dying or are bereaved. This is a book that comes from both the head and the heart. I hope I am young enough to be objective, and yet old enough to be realistic.

Others – as you will discover – have shared in the writing of this book with me. My wife Stephanie and family – especially Ruth – have been closely involved. Friends at church have helped me, and I want particularly to thank Sue and Pat, Jean and Geoffrey for all the help they have given. I have received helpful professional advice from Trevor Lambart in the course of the writing, and encouragement all the way from David Wavre of Eagle.

I have written as a Christian for others who are

Christians, but also for those who may not be sure what they believe, but are willing to listen to what Christians have to say.

We shall all face illness and death. We all have the same needs. My own personal conviction and experience is that it is the Christian hope centred in Jesus that will hold and sustain us in the valley of death and beyond. My prayer is that reading this book will strengthen the faith and hope of those who already believe, and answer questions, encourage hope and bring forth personal faith for those who join us on this journey through bereavement, but may at this moment not be sure exactly what they do believe.

May none of us be fearful of *going home*.

Michael Cole

A very personal note

The first revision of this book was completed on 2 September 1992.

That same day, our first grandson, Daniel, came home from Whipps Cross Hospital. He had spent the first three months of his very young life there and in the Special Care Baby Unit of Homerton Hospital. He was born eleven weeks early, and received great care from the hospital staff so that he might live. He brings us all great joy.

Four days later, in the same hospital, his great-grandmother, 'Nana' Speechley, eighty-six years his senior, died and went into the presence of Jesus. Some of the family were gathered around her bed that Sunday morning with great sadness and tears, and yet with peace. She, too, had gone home. Nana displayed in her life both a Martha-like concern to serve her family and her church, and also the love, peace and devotion of Mary. Like all 'Nanas' she was very special and we will miss her very much. This book is dedicated to her. One day she will know. That little cameo of family life will be repeated again and again. This book seeks to speak to the personal situations that all of us will face.

1

What Happens When I Die?

Frank sat on the edge of his hospital bed. He was wearing a green pyjama jacket and blue hospital trousers. He'd had a second heart attack. Last time I visited him in hospital we had talked about the hope that there is a life after this one. But, he was still struggling with the question 'what happens when I die?' We talked again about 'the Christian hope'. Frank turned to me and said 'I'm making an effort to believe there *is* something after death!'

On another occasion, Pam was standing in her front room, surrounded by a small daughter and a new baby son. Toys were scattered everywhere. I had gone to talk about Thomas' baptism. Instead, I found myself talking about her father's expected death from cancer. Pam was near to tears. 'It isn't fair! Why Dad, when he was just about to retire? What had he done wrong?' She was clearly angry with God, finding it hard to understand death, and to know what happens when we die.

Frank and Pam are not alone in asking the question. The famous, and the unknown, face the same question. Charles Forte, of hotel fame, wrote in his autobiography, 'And the next world? I believe, as most people I think do, in an after-life and the existence of a supreme beneficent being. But when I think of it deeply I have no concept of what that after-life can be like, or can't be like – none at all. Facing us is eternity, immortality, an experience which lies beyond the human capacity to imagine. I am more intrigued than afraid'.[1]

Charles Forte is not alone. Some 71% of people taking part in a Gallup Poll said they believed in an after-life, but were not sure what it was like.

This is not the only question people ask when facing death. Other questions include: Should we tell a person they are dying? What do I do when someone has died? Why do I feel so lonely? Will I ever get over it? Should children be sheltered from death? Is there a heaven? How do you help those who are dying? and What do you say to those who have lost loved ones? These are the questions of the heart and the mind that death raises. I want to try to answer them.

I write of death, but it can come to us in a variety of ways – the natural death of an older person, a sudden accident, a tragic suicide, an emotional abortion. However it comes, the same questions arise.

What does happen when I die?

People will give a variety of answers. I would like to mention six possible answers that you may meet in one way or another.

Some will say there is **nothing after death**. The humanist – who sees life simply in physical and material terms – believes that life has ended. The

funeral ceremony is a brief public tribute to a life
that has been, but is no more. They will admit
that mourning is very important to help those
who have lost someone they love. The mourning
process is helped by the open acknowledgement of
death, and of the difficult adjustments to life that
must follow.

A growing number of people believe in **reincarnation.** That simply means that they believe that
they come back to a further life, as a higher or
a lower being, depending upon the good or evil
life that they have lived. This belief stems from
eastern religions.

Others claim to find comfort in being able to have
some form of **spiritual contact** with departed
loved ones. It is claimed that attendance at a
seance or news from a spiritualist meeting that
our beloved is all right and has a message for the
family they have left is clearly reassuring and full
of comfort.

Others will speak of **death as release.** On the
memorial of Martin Luther King, the great black
American leader, are these simple words: 'Revd.
Martin Luther King Jr. 1929–1968 "Free at last,
free at last. Thank God Almighty, I'm free at last"'
That was a hope linked to his clear Christian faith.
For others, death is the release from all the pain
and physical limitations of this earthly life.

Others look for reassurance about death, and hope
that in the end all shall enjoy some kind of future.
That if there is a life after death, then there will

be no separation, no judgement, and that everyone will end up with God because he is a God of Love. This is a dominant British belief which is known as **Universalism**.

Some, however, believe that there is a **separation.** I recall a local Muslim doctor saying that Muslims believe in a life after death and that the quality of that life is according to the life the deceased has lived on earth.

In contrast to all this, Christians believe in the **resurrection** of the dead. Mother Teresa wrote of death as 'going home'[2] Canon Scott Holland, a former Canon of St. Paul's Cathedral in London, said 'Death is nothing at all. I have only slipped away into the next room'. A great Christian leader and friend, Major Bill Batt, looked forward to death and life with the Saviour, the Lord Jesus Christ, as 'treasure in heaven'.

I shall always remember sitting around a table with seven or eight of his colleagues as one of them read out the poem that the Major had enclosed in one of his last letters, when he knew his own death was near:

'This Earthly House'
(II Corinthians 5:1)

They tell me I am getting old but that's not really so,
The house I live in may be worn, and that of course I know.
It's been in use a good long while and weathered many a gale,

I'm therefore not surprised to find it's getting
    rather frail.

You tell me I am getting old – you mix my
    house with me –
You're looking at the outside, that's all that
    most folk see!
The dweller in the little house is young and
    bright and gay,
Just starting on a life that lasts through long
    eternal day.

The changing colour of the roof, the windows
    looking dim,
The walls a bit transparent and getting rather
    thin,
The foundation not so steady as once it used
    to be,
And that is all that you observe – but that's
    not really me.

I patch the old house up a bit to make it last
    the night,
But soon I shall be flitting to my Home of
    endless light.
I'm going to live for ever there, my life goes
    on – it's grand.
How can you say I'm getting old? You do not
    understand.

These few short years can't make me old, I
    feel I'm in my youth.
Eternity lies just ahead, full life and joy
    and truth.
We will not fret to see this house grow shabby
    day by day,

But look ahead to our new Home, which never
  will decay.

I want to be made fit to dwell in that blest
  house above,
Cleansed in the Precious Blood of Christ and
  growing still in love:
The beauty of that glorious Home no words
  can ever say,
'Tis hidden from these mortal eyes, but kept
  – for us – some day.

My house is getting ready in the land beyond
  the sky.
Its Architect and Builder is my Saviour now
  on high,
But I rather think He's leaving the furnishing
  to me,
So it's 'Treasure up in Heaven' I must store
  each day you see.

Beth Coombe Harris[3]

This is a poem full of hope and life, heaven and
resurrection. Yet it is clear that people have given
a variety of conflicting answers to the most important question of all 'What happens when I die?'
There is nothing; there is reincarnation; there is
some kind of release; there is hope for all; there
is reward of some sort; there is resurrection.

The questions we ask

It would seem that our efforts to find answers
have only produced a series of questions.

Can we possibly know what happens after death? Why do Christians believe in a resurrection? Is it wrong to try to make contact with those who have died, and to believe in some form of reincarnation? Are we just snuffed out? Will we meet our loved ones again in heaven? Will we recognise them? If there is a heaven, do we go straight there or do we have to wait? Is there paradise or purgatory? What will we do in heaven, and what will it be like? Does God care at all about death, especially if we have been praying for someone to get better and they die? I will try to answer these questions later but will end this chapter by explaining what death is.

What is death?

Death – that moment and experience when the essential physical functions of heart and brain cease to function – is described in the Bible as both an enemy and a gateway. It is separation from this life, and a union with the life to come. It is both heartache and hope. It is hell and heaven. Death is bereavement and belonging. Let me explain in more detail.

Death is like an **enemy.** Paul wrote 'For Christ must reign until he has put all his enemies under his feet. The last enemy to be destroyed is death' (1 Corinthians 15:25–26). Most people will look upon death as the enemy that separates us from those we love but not understand *why* this is the case.

The world that God made was perfect. He

planned that we should enjoy unending friendship with God our creator. For that reason God gave man instructions of what we should and shouldn't do. God also gave man choice and free will.

Sadly man decided to disobey God. As a result sin – and therefore separation – came between God and man. The end result of that disobedience and resultant separation was death.

The death that resulted was a physical death for our bodies and a spiritual death – or separation from God – for our souls. Death was thus the great enemy that Jesus had to defeat.

We shall discover later on how Christ wonderfully overcame death through his own death and resurrection. The result was to give everyone hope and life. Until we have discovered that truth, death remains the great enemy that faces everyone.

Death is likened to **wages.** This follows on from what we have just read. 'The wages of sin is death, but the gift of God is eternal life in Christ Jesus our Lord' (Romans 6:23). There wasn't going to be pain and separation and fear and evil in the perfect world that God made. However, man insisted in having his own way, and sin and death came into the world and spoilt what God had done. The result or payment for that sin was death.

Death is **a dark valley.** Psalm 23 is probably the best known and best loved psalm in the Old Testament. It reminds us that the Lord is **our** shepherd and that though we walk through the valley of the shadow of death, we need not fear

evil because our Shepherd is with us to protect
and guide and guard us.

People who have faced death know the reality
and darkness of that valley. For some, it is a very
long, deep and cold valley with little light shining
through. For others, it is more like a shadow that
passes over the sun at the end of one day, and then
lifts to reveal the brilliant light, warmth and joy
of a new day that will never end. It will be just as
if we have gone to sleep one day and woken in a
new home the next.

The New Testament also speaks of death as **sleep.**
Paul is writing about the return of Jesus and
says that some Christians will be awake and
alert when he returns. Others will be asleep in
death. 'God did not appoint us to suffer wrath,
but to receive salvation through our Lord Jesus
Christ. He died for us so that, whether we are
awake or asleep, we may live together with him'
(1 Thessalonians 5:9–10).

But death is also spoken about as the **gateway**
we go through as we set out on a new journey.
I think that I personally find this picture the
most helpful.

Jesus was speaking to his disciples and assur-
ing them about the future. He had told them he
was going away, but they didn't know where he
was going and how they could find the way. So
Jesus said to them: 'Do not let your hearts be
troubled. Trust in God; trust also in me. In my
Father's house are many rooms; if it were not
so, I would have told you. I am going there to
prepare a place for you. And if I go and prepare

a place for you, I will come back and take you to
be with me that you also may be where I am'
(John 14:1–3).

Jesus likened life to a journey. On that journey there are a number of stopping points —
rather like the service stations on the motor-
way. But just like any car journey, there is a
final destination we aim to reach. That final
destination is 'my Father's house'. We need to
go through the gateway of death to get there, but
we don't have to take that step on our own. Jesus
says that he will come back for us and take us
there himself.

So we see that the Bible shows us various pictures
of death – it is an enemy to be defeated; wages that
are paid; a valley to pass through; sleep to awake
from; a gateway into heaven and fellowship to be
found in Jesus.

For the Christian, death is that moment when
we travel from our earthly home to our heavenly
home. For everyone concerned – young and old –
death is the most certain event in life, yet one we
speak least about. It is the final journey about
which we all have questions we long to have
answered.

Wherever you are on this journey; whether you
are ill, or bereaved, or wanting to learn how to
help others, we shall have to spend some time at
the bed-side as we face illness and death. We shall
have to go to the grave-side, even though we wish
we could by-pass those days, and then we come to
the fire-side, with the chair that stands opposite
us empty. You may probably wish that somewhere
along the way you yourself could die. It seems the

easiest way out. But for the Christian there is a
better end to the journey. There is life after death.
There is heaven. There is a reunion to help ease
the pain of parting.

At the end of each chapter I have chosen a
reading from the Bible, and a short prayer that
you might like to use as you travel from one point
on the road to another. I may not have travelled
the road in exactly the same way as you are now
travelling it, but the Person who is able to meet
us along that road – the Lord Jesus Christ – is the
one who can meet us wherever we are and help
us along the journey.

A Bible Reading:

Then one of the elders asked me, "These in
white robes – who are they, and where did
they come from?"

I answered, "Sir, you know." And he said,
"These are they who have come out of the
great tribulation; they have washed their
robes and made them white in the blood of
the Lamb. Therefore, they are before the
throne of God and serve him day and night
in his temple; and he who sits on the throne
will spread his tent over them. Never again
will they hunger; never again will they thirst.
The sun will not beat upon them, nor any
scorching heat. For the Lamb at the centre
of the throne will be their shepherd; he will
lead them to springs of living water. And God
will wipe away every tear from their eyes."

(Revelation 7:13–17)

A Prayer:

Lord, I have not had to face death before, and there are many things I don't know, and many fears I can't deal with. Please give me your help and your hope as I set out on this journey through death. For Jesus' sake. Amen.

2

Ministering to the Dying

'I'm not afraid of death. But I must admit I am very apprehensive about dying with all its messiness and indignity.' That hospital patient's honest comment would be echoed by many. As a generation we do not talk about death. We try to avoid the subject, but in our minds, we know that we must all 'go' sometime. The later the better! It is some great adventure or dread in the future. We can ignore it today.

However, dying has a way of creeping up on us. It may be the sudden discovery of inoperable cancer, or the experience of a stroke or major heart attack. Life takes on a completely new perspective. We become aware of the things that really matter in life. Our personal relationships become the first concern in our thoughts. Others must carry the responsibilities we have held until that time. Life and survival is first on the agenda. Everything else fades into insignificance. We begin that last great battle in life and the enemy is death.

Does death become the uninvited intruder, or the welcome guest into a life? How the dying person reacts, and how others in the family react is going to make all the difference to the closing

months, or years, of their life here on earth. There
needs to be much understanding . . .

Be willing to talk about death

The most important reaction will be the willingness or otherwise to talk about dying, and being
able to do so with a husband or wife. Many are
the times when close relatives have told me of an
aged father who is dying, and then have added,
'but please don't say anything to him. We don't
want him upset more than need be.' Sometimes
it is a husband who tries to protect his wife, or
the wife her husband.

If we can talk about death, then we can be open
about our feelings and fears. We can say the things
that we want to make sure are said before it is too
late. It is very important to assure the dying person that they are loved. There are different ways
of doing this. A word, a gentle kiss, a soft touch
and a reassuring embrace – despite the restraints
of the hospital bed, can convey that we care.

Being willing to face the fact of dying means
that the past can be talked about freely, and the
future openly. Talk about hopes for the partner –
are they given permission to think of marrying
again? What arrangements should be made for the
finances of the family? We can even talk gently,
and sensitively, about any requests for the service.

Should we tell people they are dying?

That is a most difficult question to answer, and
there is no straightforward answer. It is an issue
that doctors, nurses and clergy face as well as the

family. The general evidence is that a minority
of people (about 30%) don't want to talk about
death in any circumstance. However, a majority
– and more than we would expect – do want to
know the truth. They feel cheated if that truth
has been kept from them. It is important to try
to assess each individual. Each patient and
person is unique, and so must be told, or not,
as we feel they themselves giving us the lead.
As one doctor working in a hospice has written,
'The doctor need have no rigid policy except to lead
where the patient leads'. I think that is sound and
sensible advice. Some people will feel cheated and
undervalued if they are not told. Some will want
to avoid the topic, whilst others will respond with
quiet hope and peace as they face dying.

A former President of the Royal College of
Physicians believed that patients fell into three
groups on this issue:

i.   Those who wish to face the facts and who
     should be allowed to do so.
ii. Those who really know the truth but prefer not
     to discuss it either to avoid embarrassment to
     the doctor, or because they prefer not to have
     their fears confirmed, and would rather be left
     with a chink of hope.
iii. Those who do not want to face the facts and
     are often patently trying to conceal the truth
     from themselves and others.[1]

Obviously great care and sensitivity has to be
excercised as to whether and when the truth
should be told, or not, depending on which cat-
egory we feel the person we are facing fits into.

The loss of dignity and privacy

This is a painful process. Everything has to be done for the patient, who no longer can wash, or go to the toilet, in private. A wretched sense of helplessness and human indignity is felt in a way that is frighteningly new. A woman cannot sit up and brush her hair, or do her make-up. A man cannot shave without help. The sufferer becomes wretched, and aware of smells and bodily reactions that can embarrass, and finds it hard to believe that those who love them will tenderly minister to them, and carry out the most menial tasks again and again without complaint, even to the changing of the sheets following heavy perspiration or incontinence.

We can sometimes add to the sense of indignity by the way that we talk at the bedside. Don't talk about the dying person as though they were not present. Remember that though they may not be able to respond in words, yet they will probably hear and understand all that is being said. Dying people have rights! The right to be heard, the right to share in any decisions about their care, the right to have the best quality of life, the right to be cared for, and the right to die when their body and spirit are ready.

Helping people face their fears

There is no denying the fact that those who are dying face real fears. There is the fear of pain and indignity; the fear – with cancer – that the disease will somehow grow and take over the whole body, even to the point of strangulation. Fear can so

easily feed on the imagination, particularly in
a hospital bed where there is a lot of time to
think. Another fear is that of waking up in the
crematorium, or of going to sleep at night afraid
of never waking again.

The fears faced in dying must be dealt with in
the same way as the fears faced in life. It is much
better to share them with those near and dear.
Sometimes those fears may seem to us, sitting by
the bedside, to be strange or almost humorous.
But to the dying person, they are very real and
personal. We must accept them in that way, and
bring the word of assurance, and allow the Lord to
take their fears away from them. There is a lovely
promise in the Psalms 'I sought the Lord and He
answered me: He delivered me from all my fears'.
(Psalm 34:4)

The fear of pain

Probably the most frequent fear is the fear of pain.
Pain can come in different forms. There is physical
pain, but also mental pain and anguish, together
with social pain and spiritual anxiety. Often these
different forms of pain are interlinked. But they
each need to be dealt with in the appropriate way.
Pain killers may ease the body, but the good news
of the Gospel will ease spiritual pain. Forgiveness
will put right wrong personal relationships.

The fear of loneliness

Next to the fear of pain is the fear of being alone
and dying alone. So friendship, security and love

are very real needs. The hours that we may have to spend sitting by a bedside, and feeling helpless, will be most important times. We may have to listen to incoherent groans, and feel desperately inadequate. We may be able to ask a few simple questions and lean forward for the whispered reply. We might just be able to wipe a perspiring forehead and body, or hold a feverish hand, or turn the radio up or down. It may be the blind that needs to be drawn or the pillow plumped up. It may be the cry for another sip of water, or the assurance that the nurse does know the bell has been rung and is coming. To you they may seem very small acts of love. To those dying they are the most important thing in all the world at that minute. Above all, it is essential that the family, and all who are near and dear come to visit to say farewell. It may just be a wife or a husband, a mother or a father who is actually there at the end. You feel there is so little you can do. But you are doing everything you need to do by being there and being available and letting the silent words of love pass between the two of you when nothing more can be said except 'Good-bye darling. God bless' and then the silent tears will fall.

Some special fears

There are a number of situations that call for special wisdom and abilities. We are an aged population in Britain. The issue of voluntary and non-voluntary euthanasia is on the public agenda. For example, in Holland in 1990, on average three people were killed each day without their consent just because they were old. People must be able to call on specialist help if they are afraid of that happening to them.

Another growing social and personal problem will be the number of people – usually younger people – who are dying as a result of infection with the HIV virus – AIDS victims. There is the horrible social stigma they face alongside the slow advance of inevitable death. But the cause of the infection may have been some infected blood given in a transfusion, and not a sign of any sexual immorality. In addition to the struggle with death that we have outlined above, some families will have to face this additional burden. Again special help is available and it needs to be asked for. It is everyone's right.

There may be the pain of life added to the pain of death for a few people, in that they know they have not been wanted all their life-time. They have felt 'in the way'. If they are honest, death will be a happy release. They will be free at last. But they are also aware that other members of the family will feel guilty and will find it hard to face their own reactions that have been suppressed all these years. Again, they will need to seek special help from their doctor, or those who can help them spiritually. I have not felt it right to explore these issues in greater depth in a book that seeks to remain as brief and as simple as possible, but we need to make passing mention of them.

Doubt

Sometimes horrible doubts come in disturbing the dying person's peace. Small events from the past come back into their mind. The arrow of doubt attacks their faith as a Christian. However much they know in their head that God loves them, in the pain of illness they don't always feel his love. After all, what is lovely about a worn-out person lying uneasily in a row of hospital beds? Doubt is best conquered by the truth, and the reminder of a simple promise from the Bible, or the directing of their thoughts to the unchanging love of Jesus will best dispel their fears and doubts.

I have tried to let feelings come to the surface at times in this book because feelings matter. That is not to deny that facts and faith don't matter, but we need to give space to all three. We are human beings as well as Christians. We have bodies as well as souls. We have tears as well as trust, and dying and death provide an occasion for both.

The process of dying

We may not always recognise what is happening to our feelings, as we watch someone die, and as we face death ourselves. We may wonder why we are reacting as we are. It might be helpful to point out that there are stages in the process of dying, just as there are in bereavement.

At first there is **denial**. 'No, not me' 'It can't be true.' 'I can't believe it, the doctors must be wrong. I'll get a second opinion – that will be better!' Then the **realisation** that the news and diagnosis is right and the denial becomes **anger** and **rage**. 'Why me? Why should "old

so and so", who doesn't do as much as I do, go
on living, when I'm dying? It doesn't seem fair
of God. What have I done wrong to deserve this?'
Then may come **bargaining with God**. If we will
spend a lot more time praying. If we will put this
or that right in our life, will God ease the pain,
or give some measure of relief? Sadly, it doesn't
work. When such a bargain is made with God it
is very rarely kept.

This inescapable truth can cause **depression**.
As Dr Elisabeth Kulber-Ross states: 'First the
person mourns past losses, things not done, and
wrong committed. When the dying patient doesn't
want many visitors that is the sign that they have
finished their unfinished business. They are now
ready to let go peacefully. So they have reached the
last stage – "Acceptance". "My time is very close
now and it's all right." This is not resignation, but
it is victory.'

Acceptance and letting go. That last stage is
very important. The dying person needs to let go,
and also members of the family need to let go.
We can sometimes hang on to people and prevent
them dying when that is really what they want
to do. Acceptance will also allow us to prepare for
death together, and begin to grieve together for
each other. That is not morbid. It is the healthy
acceptance of death. Death is no longer the last
enemy. It has become the old family friend ready
to usher the dying one into the presence of Jesus
and our Maker in heaven.

I have outlined the common problems and reactions that a dying person will face. But we need
also to consider what help is at hand.

Resources

Different cultures have different ways of marking illness, dying and death. For some, there is a great conspiracy of silence. For others, there is great openness. The family is invited to view the body. There is much wailing at the funeral. There are special and meaningful ceremonies and traditions. It would seem that the more people are allowed to share in the process of dying and death, the more they are able to accept it, and the sooner they come to terms with it. In various ways, it is the living who will help the dying.

Friends and family

The dying want to see family. Just for them to be there. Short and frequent visits are better than long and irregular ones. We need to realise that sitting on the bed may be uncomfortable for the dying. We need to sit near to them in such a position that they can see us and talk with us without any effort at all. Sometimes we may be told that the dying don't want visitors – or not very many. Friends and family mustn't be hurt by this. The ones who will most help will accept the situation as it is, without making demands. They will bring a smile, and a sense of love, care and gentleness. It is those who will understand and lift people into the presence of Jesus that are best welcomed. Friends will sometimes be able to share with the family. Luci Shaw recalled the value of having her friend Karen with her, at the time of Harold's illness. 'Karen spent most of the morning with me, waiting for the bronchoscopy to be done. Though full of people, the hospital was a lonely place. Having my friend to stay and pray with me defused some of my growing anxiety and fatigue.'[2]

A dying nurse once expressed her feelings to her fellow nurses. She reminds us just how essential our loving care and friendship is. 'I know you feel insecure, don't know what to say, don't know what to do. But please believe me, if you care you can't go wrong. Just admit that you care. That is really for what we search. We may ask for why's and wherefore's, but we don't really expect answers. Don't run away . . . wait . . . all I want to know is that there will be someone to hold my hand when I need it. I am afraid. Death may get to be routine to you, but it is new to me. You may not see me as unique, but I've never died before. To me, once is pretty unique.'[3]

It may be that some of those nurses had not yet come to terms with their own death, something which all who minister to the dying must do. As Norman Autton has written: 'Before we can minister effectively to the dying, we have to come to terms with the meaning of our own dying for not until we ourselves have worked out fully the purpose of life and the meaning of its end can we hope to be of assistance to those who find themselves in the "valley of the shadow".'[4]

The hospice movement
The modern hospice movement is linked with the name and work of Dame Cicely Saunders, who planned her first hospice in 1959. Such hospices are found in many parts of the world today. They care specifically for the dying and their families. Dame Cicely's care is based on the belief that 'You

matter to the last moment of your life and we will do all we can, not only to help you to die peacefully, but to live until you die'.

The present day hospice movement is based on the following principles:

i.   The right to control pain.
ii. The treatment of physical distress.
iii. The readiness for doctors to discuss the patient's and the family's fears with a caring attitude.
iv. The need for doctors to discuss bereavement and to care for both the patient and their family.

A group of students who visited the first hospice in its early days noticed among the patients an absence of pain and drowsiness, a sense of liveliness and peacefulness, an 'indefinable atmosphere that left you feeling that death was nothing to be worried about – a sort of home-coming.' They noted also the integration of the whole team. Patients, staff and visitors were of equal importance. There seemed to be no dividing barriers.

There was a simple, positive, holistic approach to pain and dying that helped both the patients, the families and the carers. That surely is what will best help all concerned.

The place of faith

Alongside love and care must go personal faith and prayer.

Praying with people as they come to the end of their days is a privileged ministry. Sometimes I kneel by the bed. Other times, I sit as near to the bed as I can, and hold their hand, or place my hand

reassuringly on their shoulder – the physical touch
is very important. I try to pray the prayers they
would want to pray. This is an important ministry,
because many people feel quite unable to pray to
the Lord at a time of great weakness. We can pray
for the family, and the future, as well as share any
fears with the Lord.

One very helpful means of prayer and ministry
is a simple and very short form of Holy Communion
with just the immediate family around the bed.
The tiniest crumb of bread dipped into the wine
will be a powerful symbol of the love and hope we
have in Jesus.

Praying for those who are dying is also an
essential ministry of a church. Maybe in the
early days of the illness we have felt it right to
pray for healing. That is usually right. What is
important is that we know the Lord's mind about
praying for those who are very ill. We can pray for
peace, and freedom from pain. We can pray that
all concerned will be willing to 'let go' and allow
someone in much distress to slip into the presence
of the Lord.

A verse of Scripture

Alongside our prayers for the dying can go our
reading of very well known and much loved verses
from the Bible and promises of Scripture to give
reassurance at times of uncertainty. To say the
23rd Psalm slowly or to read John 14:1–4, will
often enable the dying person to mouth the words
with us. The ministry of taped music, some simple
songs or gentle guitar music is also much appreciated and will minister to both the mind and
the spirit.

The need for peace.

What is most valued is the atmosphere of order, calm and peace within the room and the home or hospital. It will help to match the longing for peace inwardly. It may be very difficult to know peace within the body. A loved one may toss and turn in bed, trying to get comfortable. They may be in some considerable distress. We can help by ensuring there is peace around them. Above all, they will welcome peace within their hearts and minds that all is left in order for their release from this life.

I have written earlier about our hope of the resurrection, and our passport to heaven. The closing days of an earthly life are not the time for long exhortations, but can be times when the simple sharing of a personal testimony will remind someone of what they have believed, and what they have heard, and how, even now, they can simply entrust themselves to the Lord Jesus as Friend and Saviour. They will value having peace with God through Jesus, and the peace of God in their hearts. They can be assured that the future both here on earth, and also in heaven, is secure in the hands of the Lord.

The end and the beginning

The one thing, more than anything else, that the dying want is to know that someone they love will be with them when they die. We may feel very helpless and frighteningly alone as we sit holding a loved one's hand, but that will be greatest help we can offer at that time.

And so we go home. The dying have gone on ahead

of us into glory and the presence of Jesus. There to
wait for us to come later. We go back home alone
and empty. Dazed by the present. Thankful for the
past, and fearful about the future.

A Bible Reading:

Be joyful in hope, patient in affliction, faithful
in prayer. Share with God's people who are in
need. Practise hospitality. Rejoice with those
who rejoice; mourn with those who mourn.

(Romans 12: 12,13,15)

A Prayer:

We pray, gracious Father, for all those whose
earthly life is drawing to its close. Grant them
the comfort of your presence.

Relieve all distress, remove every fear, and
give them peace now and at the last, through
Jesus Christ our Lord. Amen.[5]

3

Ready to Die

'The length of our days is seventy years — or eighty, if we have the strength' (Psalm 90:10). Life expectancy in the western world is increasing. Women are expected to live longer than men. Greater emphasis is put today upon planning for a long and happy retirement. Winter holidays in the sun for the over-fifty-fives are gaining in popularity. The whole emphasis in today's world is upon enjoying life rather than on planning and preparing for death. We need to do both. Planning for death and being ready to die will make very great demands upon us and all the family emotionally and personally. It will also be the most practical and detailed thing that we can do. Take the matter of making a will.

The importance of making a will

When Tony died from inoperable cancer, leaving his widow, Jane, to bring up their young son, it was discovered that he had not left a will. Jane was left with all sorts of problems to sort out with the bank and with the solicitors. Sadly, many people delay making their will until it is too late. Solicitors assure us that 'Making a will won't kill you' and it will save a lot of heartache and trouble for the grieving relatives.

Both husband and wife should make a will. It is a simple matter, and while model forms or 'do-it-yourself' wills are available from some shops, it is best to ask for help from a solicitor to ensure that everything has been left in order.

Making a will can save legal problems later on. For example, my wife and I have a small home in France, and one of our children is adopted. The French laws of inheritance distinguish between natural children and adopted children, and unless we leave specific instructions in our wills, we will cause unnecessary problems for one of our family at the time they least could cope with it.

Making a will can save family tensions. Sadly, some families scramble for the possessions of those they love. How much better to find out in advance what each member of the family might look forward to receiving and include those specific instructions in the will. For example, which of the daughters wants Mum's engagement ring? Who will inherit the grandfather clock that has been in the family for years?

Making a will saves practical problems and means that finances can be released when a whole host of bills and accounts suddenly come through the post.

Leaving one's affairs in order

You don't have to wait until you are 'old' to make your will. Nor do you have to wait until you are retired or pensioned to leave your papers in a way that others can follow and find out all the details of insurance policies, bank passbooks, birth and marriage certificates, mortgage commitments and income tax demands, and a whole host of personal and family papers that they will need to work through. It is loving, and not morbid, to leave clear instructions about our affairs so that the sorting out of them is as straightforward as possible. Some couples choose to make their wills at the time of their marriage.

I remember calling one afternoon upon a family whose father had just died after an outstanding life. He was the most meticulous man, and seemed to think of everything – with one exception. No one could find his papers or his will. There was valuable property to be shared among the family, some of whom lived in this country and some overseas. He could have spared the family a lot of pain.

I know some people who have also left personal letters to other members of the family to be opened and read when they die. Of course the family needs to be told where all these papers have been left.

Details about the funeral

It helps to leave detailed instructions about the funeral service we would like to have for ourselves. Do we want to be buried or cremated? Are there favourite hymns to be sung? Do we want to include one of the hymns sung at the wedding? Are there particular requests about 'family flowers only'? Should there be gifts 'in memory' to a favourite Christian work or charity? Is an announcement to go in the newspapers, and are there any special

people to be advised of the death? I find it helpful
to raise these issues gently with the family when
it is clear the end of a life is coming, so that the
family have time to think. We shall have more to
say about the funeral in the next chapter.

Quite often a death will leave those left behind
numb and sometimes quite unable to make what
otherwise would be a simple decision. How much
better to have made some of those decisions
together before it is too late.

Talking about death

We have enormous difficulty in talking about
death. It is a fact of life that we shall all die.
Usually parents die before the children. Normally
a husband and wife will not both die at the same
time. It is loving to face the fact of death and by
doing so, it makes everything else so much easier
to cope with.

For example, Joe came to his grandson's baptism.
He was seriously and terminally ill. All the family
were talking to each other about death, but not to
Joe. Until we can bring death out into the open,
there will be much secrecy and pretence.

Sometimes a close family friend or a minister
can gently and sensitively talk first with one
partner, and then with the other about death,
and then raise the matter with both of them, so
that they are then able to talk together about the
subject which is often too painful for them to raise
with each other: death and the future.

When there is a willingness to accept the approach
of death, the fact of dying is made more easy.

You will be able to talk about the past. You can discuss the funeral or thanksgiving service, plan for the children, and most importantly begin to grieve and cry together. You will need to let go of one another.

Spending time together

We shall want to spend as much time as possible with each other – whether as husband and wife, parent and child, or friend with friend. No task will be too difficult, no job too menial or embarrassing where two hearts are joined by love. Nothing will matter more than giving time to those we love. Each will want to assure the other about the future. The words 'I love you' will be said many times and each time will be fresh and new. Every touch will remind us that someone else is there. Each kiss will breathe the warmth of human love into a faltering heart and body.

We shall need to provide an atmosphere of quietness, warmth, love and assurance.

We shall need to assure the one cared for that they are not a burden. We shall need to remind them again and again that it is no trouble to 'go downstairs again' to attend to whatever is needed.

Every day will be a precious day. Time may seem to have stopped and we shall need to make the most of it. Other activities and concerns will need to be given a low priority. It is the chance to make sure that we have said to each other all the things that we hoped one day to be able to say. The thoughts and love locked away in our hearts will now somehow find a way to be expressed.

Finding spiritual help

It is not always easy to read the Bible or to pray during illness or when someone we love is dying. We may have the time, but we are using all our energies to help us cope.

Friends and relatives can help here. It is a real blessing to read a few very familiar and well-loved verses that feed both soul and mind. It is a help to pray short and personal prayers with them and for them. We shall need to reassure the Christian that God does understand their weakness and knows that however much we want to pray and tell him that we love him, we are just not always able to do that.

The help of friends

Close friends will have a valued part to play. Some will help with practical tasks, doing the shopping, providing a meal or coping with some other errand. Others will pass the latest news bulletin around so that the family are not constantly answering the telephone and repeating the same news again and again. Some may be able to look after other members of the family whether they are elderly relatives or young children, or take the dog for a walk if there is no one else to do it.

Around us the rest of the world will continue. The T.V. news bulletins will remind us that another day has passed, another bomb exploded, another crisis reached. And yet none of this will seem to matter. Illness and death have become all absorbing to everyone involved.

Caring for yourself

Those who are caring for others will also need to care for themselves. It can be a very tiring business sitting by a bedside, possibly waiting and wondering what you can do to help. Sleep may have been in patches. If you are able to sleep in the same bed, you lie awake not wanting to disturb the one near by. You don't feel you have done much, but you are frankly exhausted. It is not unloving to make sure you get essential brief breaks and try to eat. A short walk, a breath of fresh air, a change of surroundings and contact with familiar routine, are all helps to those who have to watch and wait. It is important, on the road to heaven, to recognise that those who go on ahead and those who will follow later both have real, but different needs as death approaches.

Some awkward questions

Questions will also arise. 'Why is this happening?' 'Could we have done anything differently?' 'Is this our fault?' 'How will I cope when my partner dies?' 'What more can I do to help?' 'Lord give me patience!' We may not get all the answers at this stage – as death comes. What God does answer, however, is the cry for his help and grace for each day. It is when we are at our most weak and vulnerable that we discover God's care and love for us day by day.

Accepting death

Just as a young family gets ready to welcome a new life, so equally a wise family will prepare for

a life to slip away into the presence and glory of
God. Just as we say 'Hello', so we need to say
'Goodbye'. We must let go and allow the hands
of Jesus to take to himself the one whose hands
have meant so much to us.

Grieving

It may sound hard to think of all this before
death, but it will make the process of grieving
and recovery after death just that bit less painful
to face. Other members of the family will need to
say their goodbyes. There may be matters to put
right and to ask forgiveness over. Much better that
this is faced now in this life, rather than leaving
it too late and finding ourselves wishing we had
dealt with it while we could.

C. S. Lewis once said: 'God whispers to us in
our pleasures, speaks to us in our conscience, and
shouts to us in our pain'.[1] In the pain of illness,
death and separation, we can know the presence
of God, and hear the voice of God. It was King
David who wrote: 'Even though I walk through
the valley of the shadow of death, I will fear no
evil, for you are with me, your rod and your staff
they comfort me' (Psalm 23:4).

The closing moments of life

The closing moments of life are most sacred and
precious. For that reason you will probably want
to spend them along with the one who is dying, or
with those very near and dear to you. You will feel
the world has stopped. You are together, and yet
you are alone. You are awake and yet exhausted.

You hold hands, and yet you feel cut off. Your mind is numb. You want to cry, but the tears won't come.

It is for this moment that together you made sure all the papers and documents were in order, that you shared your feelings and hopes about the past and for the future. It was for this moment, and for the future, that you were able to speak about death and firmly hold on to your faith about the resurrection of the dead. For one of you life will go on, but you are not sure that you want it to. For the other life on earth has ended, and yet another life has just begun.

As you look at the bed you know it is your husband or wife, your son or daughter whose body lies there, and yet their spirit has left the body. The real them is no longer present. You must now prepare for the funeral. You call for the nurse, or phone the doctor, and arrange for the local funeral director to come. Suddenly your life is taken over by all the things you have got to do but none of which you want to do.

A Bible Reading:

For to me, to live is Christ and to die is gain. If I am to go on living in the body, this will mean fruitful labour for me. Yet what shall I choose? I do not know! I am torn between the two: I desire to depart and be with Christ, which is better by far.

(Philippians 1: 21–23)

A Prayer:

O Lord, support us all the day long of this troublous life, until the shadows lengthen, and the evening comes, and the busy world is hushed, the fever of life is over, and our work is done. Then, Lord, in thy mercy, grant us safe lodging, a holy rest, and peace at the last, through Jesus Christ our Lord. Amen.[2]

4

The Funeral

It is the day that no one looks forward to, and the day that many people dread. So, how best can we prepare for the funeral, and what will help us to get through the day? I hope this chapter will answer some of those questions.

If you have never had to arrange a funeral, the question will probably arise – 'What do I do?' The best answer is to contact the funeral director you want to act for you and also your church minister. Just as a midwife helps to bring a life into this world, so the role of the funeral director is to take a life that has ended out of this world.

Registering the death

In the first few days there are many practical arrangements to make. The death must be registered. The registrar will need to have the date and place of birth, and date and place of death; the full name and the maiden name of a married woman, the last permanent address, and occupation. They will need to have details of any state pension and allowances. They will also require supporting documents such as the doctor's certificate of the cause of death. If there has to be a post-mortem, then a coroner's 'Form 100' will be sent directly to the registrar.

All this may sound rather complicated and unfeeling at a time when the last thing you want to do is to deal with forms and paper work, but remember that the people you are having to see will be aware of your feelings. They will understand the tears that begin to trickle down your cheek and the difficulty in remembering where you put things when you were quite sure you brought the papers etc. with you. It is especially helpful, if possible, to have a close friend or another member of the family to come with you, and to drive you to the different places you have to go. It will reduce the time spent in travelling, and it will be company for you at a very lonely time.

There are various circumstances in which people die – suddenly, overseas, at home, in hospital – and the procedures vary slightly. Much detailed information is available either from the Social Security Offices (their booklet is called 'What to do after a Death' D49) or from the Consumers Association, Caxton Hill, Hertford SG13 7LZ ('What To Do When Someone Dies').

The cost of the funeral

A very common feeling in planning the funeral is to want the very best for the loved one who has died. That is only right and proper. We don't always realise what costs will be involved in planning even a very simple service, so it is wise to ask the funeral director for an estimate for all that they are providing – the service, the cremation or cemetery fees, church fees, certificates, costs for the cars, any notices in the press, etc. Even though you may have an insurance policy, the money may be less than the costs you will incur. There is a tendency to overspend. This is natural, but it is not always wise, and it is not necessary. Be open with the funeral director and this will help to avoid future shock and embarrassment.

It is important that you let people know when someone had died. You will want to tell the immediate family. They will pass the news on to friends, a notice in the paper will be helpful, letters written to others who may not know, but who will want to come to the service, will all have to be dealt with. In return you will begin to receive by hand, or post, cards and letters from family, friends and neighbours. Each note will be a help to you. It will remind you of the love and care of others. They will write of the one who has died, and each word will help to bring a loved one closer to you. Their words will warm and encourage your heart, and provide a bridge across the yawning gap of loss. They will bring you tears and deep grief, but also comfort, and when you re-read them in months to come, they will again bring you closer to the person who has died.

Those letters and cards are very important. At this moment you are on the receiving end. When, however, the time comes for you to write such cards or letters to a friend or a member of the family, the time spent in choosing your words carefully, and recalling events or expressing your appreciation of the life and work of their loved one will be deeply treasured and valued. There

is an important ministry in writing letters of
sympathy.

The value of flowers

Flowers also have an important ministry. They
speak of life and colour and care and love. Flowers
in the home help to replace the emptiness that has
suddenly descended. Flowers also have a special role
for the immediate family at the funeral in the church
or chapel and on the coffin. They are a simple and
powerful symbol of deep love and affection.

However it is not always felt that lots of money
spent on other flowers is the best tribute to a
friend who has died. I find, increasingly, that
people prefer to give money in memory of people
to such work as that of the hospice movement,
missionary work, work among children, cancer
research etc. Sometimes a lasting memorial is
given in the name of a husband or wife, and
remains for years to come, a fitting and useful
tribute to someone now with the Lord.

The service you plan is for the living as well as
for the one who has died. It will be an essential
step along the road of 'letting go' and of saying
'goodbye'. For that reason it is right to have
the coffin in church. As Canon Norman Autton
has written: 'A funeral is a rite of passage, a
formal public enactment of a deeply significant
life-change. It gives the bereaved permission to
grieve and redirect their lives, and calls those
who know them to acknowledge and respect their
new status'.[1]

Thus great care should be given to planning the
service. Sometimes the details have been worked

out well in advance, the one who has died having left instructions in their will about hymns, readings, burial or cremation etc. It might have been possible, knowing that death is near, for a couple to talk together about what they would like at the service.

The following extract from a friend's letter reflects the importance of hymns. 'I remember vividly when Mum first heard this hymn at a service in church. My husband (to whom I had just become engaged) already knew it well, and she was very impressed with his lusty singing of it(!) and always loved it after that. I must share with you that it has been like a shower of sweet rain to my soul to meditate, as I've typed, on the words of these hymns and psalms. I hadn't realised fully how desperately bruised and parched and dry my spirit had become during this protracted time of closely watching my Mum and Dad suffer so deeply. It's just as well I did not use an ink pen as I think the words would have been smudged with tears.'

Allow others to help

It is important to let people help you at a time like this. Some will ask if there is shopping they can get in, others might wonder whether you want some help with a bit of cleaning, or with preparing some refreshments and cups of tea for people after the service. We don't always find it easy to receive help from others, especially if we are the independent type, but you will find you haven't got the energy to do everything you want to, and the help of friends will be invaluable.

Feelings will be very important, and at times our reactions may take us by surprise. I recall visiting some close friends whose father had died suddenly and they were travelling some hundreds of miles for the service. I just dropped in to talk about the service and their plans. Later I received this letter: 'The hug, prayer together and opportunity to just talk over the service very informally were a real help to us both. Everything was much more formal and restrained, with feelings very much hidden. I think I would have felt really disappointed if we hadn't had the opportunity we had with you to just talk freely and express our emotions'.

Another close friend wrote to me about the love she received from her Christian friends before the death of her husband – 'My thanks go to everyone for giving us the love and confidence to be able to share. This has been an immense help to me personally and I hope that people will be able to bear with my still wanting to share, because for me the pain is just beginning'. These last few words are ones we really need to hear, because the person who was the closest to the one who has died may not have allowed themselves to feel the very real physical pain of grief and bereavement until after the death.

I quote those two letters because in the midst of activity there is the need for love and to be aware of people's feelings. It is very easy for a conspiracy of silence to operate, and no one speaks of the one who has died for fear of hurting the family and friends, when what is wanted more than any other thing is to talk of a wife or husband, Mum or Dad.

In all the events leading up to, and including the day of the funeral three groups of people will be very important. Let me identify them.

i) The funeral directors

Firstly the funeral directors. As already mentioned, they will take the whole responsibility for organising and equipping the funeral. The care of the deceased entrusted to them is regarded as a 'sacred duty'. They will look after the body as if it was one of the family. I have read through the detailed manual they have. They are trained for a whole variety of different situations. They know how to act for various Christian services – whether Church of England or House Church, Brethren or Roman Catholic, (each will have its different traditions and customs). They must know the law for every circumstance. They will deal with all the paper work. They will know what to do if there is an autopsy or post mortem, or if organs are left for medical research. They will advise about the collection and disposal of ashes. They will explain the various costs and services that are available. They will know what to do whether the death takes place just round the corner from them in daytime, or overseas at night. The funeral director has a most difficult and sensitive task to perform, but a qualified funeral director will be someone on whom you can rely for help, when you feel so helpless.

ii) The clergy

The second group of people I hope you can rely on will be the local clergy. If you are a regular

member of a church, then you will be known to
your clergy, and you should make sure that they
are asked to conduct the service for you. It is what
should happen, and it is what the clergy and pas-
tors will want to happen. We want to share the
sacred moments of life and death with members
of our congregations.

If you are not linked with a church, you may
find either your local vicar or the rota clergyman
taking the service. Sometimes I hear stories that
appal me, of the insensitive manner in which my
fellow clergy have conducted a service. I hope
we are going to have fewer and fewer of those
occasions. If I am asked to take the funeral of
someone I don't know, there are certain things I
try to find out – either through a pastoral call if
they live nearby, or a phone call if the next of kin
live in another part of the country.

I ask about the person who has died. I make sure
I have their name right, and the name by which
people present at the service will know them. I
ask for the names of the immediate family and
mourners, in order of seniority, so that I can pray
personally by name for them during the service.
I find out who will be present, how they will
think of the friend who has died. We talk about
any hymns. I hope to be able to say something
of the hope we have in the Lord Jesus. I pray
with the bereaved as we anticipate the service. It
is vital that I put myself in their place, and speak
personally and sensitively of the person they all
knew so well.

I mention this aspect of the day of the funeral,
because the family might wonder why the clergyman or minister is wanting to know all these

things. It is in order that we should help people
to grieve and to let go of the one who has died.

iii) Family & friends

The third group of people who can help or hinder
us on the day of the funeral is the immediate
family and friends. The ideal is that each sup-
ports the other. Sometimes the funeral – like a
wedding or a baptism – is the one occasion when
the members of the family meet each other. It is a
time of sorrow, and a time of greeting and catching
up on the news. There can be all sorts of personal
reactions and 'vibes' that are present. Some may
be living in denial, pretending that 'Mum' or 'Dad'
hasn't died, and the sight of the coffin is a stark
and silent reminder that a death has happened.
There may be awkward relationships and unresolved tensions that are running just beneath the
surface. 'X' doesn't understand, 'Y' hasn't spoken
to 'Z' for years. We need to understand and help
each other, being willing to talk of the one who
has died. A funeral should draw a family closer
together. Sometimes it is a witness of deeper
family tensions and divisions.

Some friends may be nervous about calling,
phoning, or troubling the family. The important
thing is to make contact in the most helpful and
sensitive way. Avoiding the family or friend at this
time only adds to the hurt.

Children

I have said nothing throughout this chapter about
children and younger members of the family. They
are as important as the grown ups. They should be

allowed to be there. There is sometimes a feeling
that we should shield children from death and
keep them away on the day of the funeral. But
children have feelings like their parents do. They
need to grieve like grown ups. They are just as
bereaved of a Mum as Dad is bereaved of his wife.
Because children and young people are so important, I have devoted a whole chapter (chapter 7) to
the theme of death for the children, and the death
of a child.

Practical issues

If the day of the funeral is dreaded, then the days
after the funeral are even more difficult. They can
be empty and very long. The day after the funeral
is the first day of the rest of life that at this stage
doesn't seem to be worth living. So there are some
important things to note.

Getting a **good night's sleep** is something that is
important, but which may not have been possible
for weeks or months beforehand. You are tired out,
physically and emotionally, and completely empty.
The inner batteries of the spirit are run down. It
may be wise to consult your doctor to ask for a
mild sedative in order to get some undisturbed
sleep. What seems wise to avoid is a tranquillizer
that is so strong that your reactions are dulled,
and you find that feelings are blanketed out and
you are robbed of memories and experiences that
you might have treasured.

It is sensible to plan just **one day at a time**.
Sometimes a person can only think a morning

or an hour ahead. You wonder how on earth you are going to cope with the future that stretches threateningly into the distance. 'Take one day at a time' seems to be the right guideline.

Don't make hasty decisions – and certainly not on major matters such as those connected with your home, your money or your future. If you are invited to spend some time with other members of the family or with friends, then don't put off the day when you will need to come back into the home by yourself and face the future. I know there will be lots of clearing up and tidying out to do, but that can wait. Give yourself permission to do as little or as much as you feel you want to do. There will however, be some decisions you will have to bear in mind following the funeral. There will be letters of thanks to write for example, but don't feel you have to tackle the pile all in the first week. Do what you can when you can.

At this stage you will still feel numb and without any energy. Other members of the family, and even your close friends, will get back to their routine again very quickly and they may fall into the trap of thinking that you can too. What they forget is that you will never get back to the old routine. Life and relationships have drastically altered, and you have to begin making a new life for yourself and possibly for the children, and that is going to take months and years. It is about that and the long-term reactions that we shall look at in the next chapter.

There will be the temptation to sit up late, dozing in front of the fire or aimlessly watching television because there is nothing better to do.

It will be essential that you begin to take care of yourself now. You have taken care of others and loved them. Now is the time for you to love yourself, to look after your sleeping and eating and to begin to rebuild your life.

There will be unanswered questions and unfinished conversations that the death has posed. There will be the 'if onlys', 'if only I had done this or not said that'. Try to put such thoughts on one side, so that you can deal with them when you find your mind is clearer, and your emotions more in check.

There may be those times when you wish you had told the one who has died that you were sorry about something and now you feel it is too late. Some people have found it helpful to use prayer at this point to ask Jesus to 'pass a message on' to a loved one, and in that way some unfinished personal and emotional business can be completed.

The funeral was a very personal, public and formal occasion of saying farewell to a loved one. Friends and family shared together in the event. It was important to give time and effort to planning the details. You have wanted the very best.

Suddenly you may find yourself surprised that, against every expectation, you 'enjoyed' the day in a strange way. The service and all that happened was a proper tribute to a husband or wife or colleague. They were very close to you in all that happened. The day you were dreading might have turned out to be a real help.

Friends have supported you, the family have gathered round, tributes have been expressed, prayers have been answered, and your faith has been helped and encouraged.

But now you have to face the future, and it is to that we shall turn.

A Bible Reading:

When the Jews who had been with Mary in the house, comforting her, noticed how quickly she got up and went out, they followed her, supposing she was going to the tomb to mourn there. When Mary reached the place where Jesus was and saw him, she fell at his feet and said, 'Lord, if you had been here, my brother would not have died'. When Jesus saw her weeping, and the Jews who had come along with her also weeping, he was deeply moved in spirit and troubled. 'Where have you laid him?' he asked. 'Come and see, Lord', they replied. Jesus wept. Then the Jews said, 'See how he loved him!'

(John 11: 31–36)

A Prayer:

Lord Jesus, you spoke words of comfort to your friends Martha and Mary in their time of sorrow, so please keep and comfort us as we mourn today. May we find our peace and hope and strength in you, the Resurrection and the Life, for your tender mercies' sake. Amen.[2]

5

Unexpected Reactions

Life returns to normal for everyone, except you.
Two or three weeks after the funeral, everyone else is back to their familiar routine, but that
is not true for you. Your child does not return from
school at 4.00pm. Your husband does not come
home from work at 6.30pm. You begin to discover
a whole range of unexpected reactions developing
within yourself. I want to try to describe some of
those reactions in this chapter.

Three things, however, must be said by way of
introduction. First, not everyone's experience of
death will be the same. The death may have been
the result of a heart attack, or a road accident. It
may have been be the result of a cot death or a
suicide. It may have been peaceful or savage and
cruel. Maybe it was expected or sudden. The dead
person may have been young or very old. You may
have been close to them and very dependent, or
you might even be slightly relieved that the death
has taken place.

Secondly, because of the varied ways in which
bereavement comes to us, we shall find that we
have a variety of emotions ranging from peaceful thankfulness to guilty panic. From prepared
acceptance to sheer disbelief. Because of this, the

land of sorrow through which we shall have to travel may be different for us from the experience of others.

Thirdly, however, the journey we shall take will have some common features, and it is that journey through bereavement that I want to try to share with you, so that you recognise the landmarks when you pass through the valley of the shadow of death.

It is important that we understand ourselves. We need to know ourselves, help ourselves, love ourselves, learn to pray again for ourselves and to live with ourselves. Some will be tempted to deny or suppress their feelings, but that will only delay the God-given, built-in recovery programme.

When someone very near and dear has been taken from us we feel robbed, desolate and empty. It is natural that we mourn and grieve. Tears are a God-given means of emotional release. We hurt ourselves if we deny our feelings. It is those who mourn, said Jesus, who shall be comforted. (Matthew 5:4)

Let me share two people's reactions. Luci Shaw describes how she felt the day after her husband Harold's funeral. 'I came down with flu, but got out of bed to see Terry today. I described to her my lack of emotion: Why am I not feeling more pain or the grief of Harold's departure? She (friend Terry) thinks I have been grieving all year, preparing for death, learning to accept the inevitable separation.'[1] There are some important experiences mentioned in that short extract — numbness, grieving, and acceptance.

A friend to whom Stephanie and I have been very close before and since the death of her

husband, wrote down her feelings and thoughts
a few months after Mike's death. 'Life seems very
pointless now, nothing seems important apart
from my own grief and sadness. I often feel very
selfish and inward-looking, as if wallowing in my
own misery. I suppose that other things in life
will take on importance again, and I will even
feel happy, but just at the moment it's difficult
not to feel guilty or disloyal to be enjoying things
in life again, or even not thinking about Mike for
a while. I feel I have suffered a loss of identity, no
longer being a part of a couple, no longer "Mike's
wife", but now his widow. I miss someone to love
and who loves me.

'At the moment I am allowing myself the time
and the "permission" to grieve for as long as I
feel the need, and trying not to feel pressurised by
others. People have suggested to me that "Christians don't grieve", but I am sure that it is natural
to grieve and even dangerous to suppress it. Death
is after all a physical separation from someone we
love, and that is desperately sad in human terms,
whether we are a Christian or not. Yet I could not
cope without my Christian hope, and that of being
reunited in Christ.

'In the last few weeks of Mike's life, and these
past weeks since his death, I have found it very
difficult to pray, and felt very dry spiritually. I
have just had to rely on others doing my praying
for me for a while, as I have been able to do little
more than pray for strength for just one day at a
time, both leading up to and since his death. I have
learnt to be vulnerable, and not to be ashamed or
embarrassed to let others see me cry. It's easy to
assume that I'm the only person who has ever

suffered such deep grief, but I know that others must have felt as desolate as I, and yet have come through it. It's like a journey through a long dark tunnel, and it is good to know that there will be light at the end of that tunnel eventually.'

You may well identify with those reactions and thoughts. They are full of reality and they breathe hope into our sorrowing hearts. What therefore is this pattern or process of grief that bereaved people pass through? It may help if I set out very simply the stages we all go through. What is not so easy is to suggest the time we each take to travel that particular part of the road. For some it is a journey that takes months, for others years. What must be made clear is that the end of the journey is acceptance and rebuilding of our life, and yet the end of the journey doesn't bring us back to where we were before death entered our life, but rather further down the road of life.

The journey to recovery

i. We all begin with a sense of shock and denial

We just can't believe it has happened. We are numb inside. Physically we feel weak and limp, and yet we are tense and on edge. Everything is remote and unreal. We still expect the person to walk into the room as usual. We think we hear their voice. Our heads tell us that someone has died, but our hearts and emotions are in shock and have not yet caught up with the facts.

ii. A mixture of fantasy and unreality follow linked with a sense of anger

We are tempted to bargain with God, though we know in our hearts that that won't accomplish anything.

iii. We begin to blame the doctors or nurses who were caring for our loved one

We try to reason that he or she would not have died if certain events had or had not happened. We don't see the point of our going on living, and may even ask God to take us as well.

iv. Then we suddenly feel guilty

We are only too aware that there were lots of things we could have done together, things we wish had not happened, or had happened. We feel unworthy of the one who has died. We are quite sure we have let them down, and we long to withdraw from the real world into the darkness and isolation of our own feelings and life. We can't cope with death, the future, and ourselves. Not unnaturally that leads on to . . .

v. A sense of depression

Physically and emotionally, spiritually and mentally we find ourselves enveloped in the dark cloud of depression and we can't see any way out from it. There is no point in living. This is only made worse as the full realisation that the death is true and real begins to dawn, but then there begins to shine a glimmer of light at the end of the dark tunnel.

vi. We begin to be able to cry

There is the release of tears and the flood of grief breaks. The pain increases and is often very physical, as if our inside is being torn out. We begin to understand and cope with the pain. We begin to accept the memories of the past, and to make very simple plans for the present and the future. **We begin the process of acceptance**. Someone I love has died. I can't bring them back to me. I must accept they have died, and I must now begin to live the rest of my life without them.

That pattern of shock, anger, guilt, depression and acceptance may vary in some details for each of us, but that is the valley through which we shall have to travel. It is along that road that we shall begin to learn to help ourselves back into life.

Helping yourself

It is one thing to have some understanding of ourselves and how you will react to each situation, it is quite another thing to help yourselves through that journey and to begin to build a new life.

i. You need to 'let go' of the one who has died. Bereavement can be like living in a prison cell with the door wide open. In one way you now have a new freedom. There is an independence you long ago sacrificed, but you are held back from using it until you have learned to let go of the past. For example, you choose not to take your favourite walk because you always took that walk together. You refuse to accept the invitation of friends because it would mean going alone.

You don't go to church because you always went together and sat in the same seats. You keep the room exactly as he or she would want it to be and it becomes a shrine instead of your home. In many ordinary and subtle ways you can allow yourself to be held back by the past instead of letting go.

For example, a friend's aunt lived on a farm in Australia. After her father died, she could not face going into the local town and meeting people. Many weeks later when she did at last go into the town she felt bereaved all over again because nobody now spoke to her about her father. It is wise to face the world in stages, as soon as you feel it is possible.

Another example of this difficulty to face the facts and to face the world is seen in the butcher's shop on the High Road in my parish. The butcher died more than ten years ago, but his mother has left the window exactly as it was the day her son died. The shop has not opened, nor has the business been sold. She is finding it incredibly difficult to let go, and to begin to live her life again. Of course, there is great pain in letting go, but through the pain and letting go will come the healing.

ii. You help yourself by knowing how to react to other people. There are two main reactions you may expect to meet. One is the failure of other people to talk about the person who has died for fear of hurting you, when in fact he or she is the one person you long to talk about. You will help yourself by naturally introducing their name and life into the conversation. The other failure is the well-meaning but unhelpful comment or question such as 'It'll do you good', 'It'll get you out of the house', and worst of all 'Are you feeling better now?' You will help yourself by realising that those who have not yet passed through the pain of death won't know how insensitive such comments are. We need to learn patience, and the ability to refuse to take on board the thoughts behind the comments or questions.

iii. You help yourself by beginning to plan again for the business of everyday living. You may need to cope with personal finances in a way you have never done before. All the details and paper work may seem overwhelming. It can be at this point that friends who have more experience – like Christian accountants in the church – can be a real help. On the other hand, it may be the younger widower who has the task of cooking for himself. At first you are tempted to feel 'why bother?', 'what's the point?', 'why tidy up the house?', 'why not just eat the bits that are left over in the fridge?', 'why bother to iron the shirt?' You will find that if you give way to this temptation, your sense of self-worth will weaken and that you are not thereby helping yourself. In a church or a kindly neighbourhood, or even through books in the library, there is help of all sorts at hand as you tackle the tasks you have never had to do before. You may begin to find that you need to – and want to – tackle new interests and learn new skills. I shall say more about this in a later chapter, but it is all part of building a new life and helping ourselves and loving ourselves.

iv. You help yourself by being aware of the dangers bereavement brings. Life is full of stressful situations. Among the most common is illness, a change of job, divorce, possessing large mortgages, and holidays, but top of the list every time is the experience of bereavement. That is the most stressful situation any one of us can face, even more painful, surprisingly, than divorce. It is very easy to turn to the wrong kinds of relief when you face the stress of bereavement. You might start to drink or drink too much. Smoking might be the escape route, over-eating may be used to dull the pain and relieve the boredom, tranquillisers may be resorted to in order to help you sleep. You might embark on an unadvisable spending spree! All these things – and others as well – such as unhelpful sexual fantasies, are understandable, but they won't help you help yourself.

Fortunately, there are some very positive steps you can take to deal with such stress. Keeping physically fit – possibly by walking the dog, or some regular swimming or other activity – will be essential. Having a regular sleep pattern, and going to bed by the clock, rather than when you feel like it; regular and right eating, rather than eating when you feel hungry or can be bothered to make yourself something. All these practical steps will increase your sense of well-being and maintain a good and positive self-image. You will also find help through a living faith and a positive spirit within.

Some enemies

There will be some 'enemies' we shall have to deal with following bereavement, and it will be good to recognise them. There may be the unexpected thought of suicide, the nagging accusation of guilt and the relentless question of forgiveness and its related unanswered questions of 'what if' and 'if only'. How do we handle these issues so that we learn to help ourselves?

a) The need to forgive

I once met a young student teacher, named Jill. She was unable to feel or to express love. Her parents had divorced when she was eleven, and she was given responsibility for three younger brothers and sisters. Later her father was to die of cancer. She hated him for what he had done to the family, her mother and to herself, and she was hurting and unable to forgive him. Gently, but firmly, I had to show her that unless she was willing to forgive him – though dead – she would be hurting herself for the rest of her life. She felt it was too late and she thought it impossible to let go her anger and hostility. I asked if I might put my arms around her, as a symbol of the love that Christ has for her. Slowly she began to put her arms around me in some kind of response to that love. Her body began to relax and the tears began to flow, and she sobbed from deep within herself. Then I asked her to think of me as her father, and was she now able to forgive him, and understand why he had acted as he did. Hesitatingly, but surely, she spoke out words of forgiveness and love in a way she had never been able to do before. Her head began to lift, her eyes began to light up, and her heart began to have a lightness and joy in it as never before. That experience has been repeated in many lives in one form or another as people seek to forgive those they once knew.

b) Guilt
Guilt is often linked with forgiveness. We may have become impatient with the pain and suffering a loved one was facing. We may have felt powerless to help, and frustrated that we could do nothing. The sheer physical pain of the sufferer made them snap at us and we answered back in a way we now regret. Then they died. We now live with guilt. I am sure it is helpful to share these situations with a close Christian friend or pastor, and to confess those areas of guilt and hear the reassuring words of forgiveness and cleansing. 'If we confess our sins he is faithful and just and will forgive us our sins and purify us from all unrighteousness.' 1 John 1:9 It may be too late to ask for human forgiveness, but it is never too late in this life to ask for the Lord's forgiveness and peace to guilty souls.

c) Thoughts of suicide
These are not unnatural. Depression and the sense of emptiness together with the lack of purpose we experience are the seed-bed in which the thoughts of suicide take root. Ending it all does seem the simplest way out. But you know that we are all made in the image of God. He has given us the gift of life and to end that life and mar that image is forbidden in the Bible. It would be a very selfish act. Suicide may solve your problems, but it will leave hurt, guilt and great sadness for your family and the friends who are left. Suicide is an

expression of self-hatred, and what we are aiming at is self-love.

Loving yourself

You have spent a great deal of your time, thoughts and energy loving someone else. You have had little time and energy for yourself. You are tired, you have not had time to go to the hairdresser's, you feel all behind with jobs in the home, and you see yourself as a bit of a wreck. Added to that you have suddenly lost part of your identity. You were a wife, now you are a widow. You were a husband and now you are a widower. You did have a family, and now you are alone. You once relied on your parents, now that generation has passed on.

The situation is made more painful by the fact that computerised mail is still delivered to the one who has died, and we want to cry out from within, 'Don't they know they've died'. We are faced with impersonal forms. A loved one has become just a number. We start to receive payments from Social Security and pension funds that may help financially but drain us emotionally. Even credit cards are no longer valid if the one who has died was the principal cardholder. (But it is important to realise that we can still operate a joint bank account even though it was opened in joint names.)

Three things will help us to love ourselves. One major relationship hasn't changed at all. I still matter very much to God and to Jesus. I am still the person he loves, died for, and befriends day by day. I still find my identity and acceptance in Jesus. I still belong to Jesus, and Jesus still belongs to me. My earthly identity may have changed, but my heavenly identity is unchanged.

Secondly, I still live in a community, and if I am a Christian I still belong to my church and fellowship, and small fellowship group, and it may be that I have discovered the love and support and daily care of my brothers and sisters in Christ in a new and deep way. I am loved and wanted for myself and I know that I matter to my friends and family.

Thirdly, I am still a member of the community socially. My role may have changed, but my belonging has not ended. I still go to the shops, visit the library, get on the bus, buy my newspaper and call at the bank. I begin to discover that I am still alive and a person. I am loved by God, and God wants me to love myself.

Sadly, many Christians have been taught that it is wrong to love themselves. We had always to be available to others. We had to deny our own needs. But Jesus loved himself. He didn't always respond to the pressing needs of others. He withdrew to renew his inner life. He had time for himself and his vital relationship with the Father, and as we learn to love ourselves, so we shall be more and more fully human and, incidentally, more and more able to serve others.

As you begin to love yourself so you will begin to pray for yourself.

Caring for yourself spiritually

Because of the sheer pressure of events and the exhaustion you have faced, you may have found

prayer almost impossible. It has been the well-
loved familiar passages of the Bible, or Scripture
verses displayed on a card that has fed your soul.
It is the knowledge that others are praying for you
that have taken the place, mainly, of you praying
for yourself. Now you want to get back to some
spiritual discipline yourself. May I make some
practical suggestions:

a) Set yourself a simple target to start with. If you
once set aside thirty minutes to read your Bible
and pray, why not start with ten, and then you will
find you increase that gradually and naturally.

b) Decide which Sunday service will best help you
as you start back at church. Can you take a big
noisy service, or would it be best to go to a smaller,
quieter mid-week service of Communion?

c) Allow the ministry of tapes – whether music or
a talk – to feed your soul in the quietness of your
own home.

d) Select the short lightweight book that minis-
ters to your need. Choose the book you want to
read, not the one you feel you ought to read or
even the books that well-meaning friends insist
you tackle.

e) Ask one or two close friends to pray with you
and for you.

f) Accept the fact that there will be times – very
special times – when you will want to visit the
grave or some special spot to feel near to a loved

one and thank God for them, or just to pray for
yourself. After all, the Gospels tell us that Mary,
who was close to Jesus, was standing there at the
tomb, weeping, and perhaps aware in her spirit of
the Lord, without at that time being aware that
he had risen.

All these 'recovery' steps – knowing yourself,
helping yourself, loving and praying for yourself
are vital, but the most difficult is the last we come
to, and that is:

Living with yourself and
by yourself

Loneliness is the great pain and burden of bereavement, and we need to face it. Out of her experience,
Luci Shaw describes this loneliness for us.

'No more. There will be no more long car trips
– he driving, me knitting . . . no more kneeling
side by side at the Communion rail, no more
warm closeness in bed on winter nights in our
flannel nightshirts, secure against the chill of the
outside world. No more love-making, and after,
sleep. No more.'[2] The point is reinforced as Luci
Shaw quotes Gerald Brenan 'The great thing
about marriage is that it enables one to be alone
without feeling loneliness. Widowhood proves the
converse – even when we're not alone, we feel
lonely to the core. Bereavement, death, is radical
surgery on a marriage. Now the anaesthiesia is
beginning to wear off. The nerves tingle, the pain
reflexes twitch. I am beginning to feel the rawness
of amputation.'[3]

But she was helped by a letter from Elizabeth

Elliot, in which Elizabeth quotes Amy Carmichael:
'All that was ever ours is ours forever'. That is
true but as Ingrid Trobisch says 'grief is the price
of loving'. Similarly 'Loneliness is the poverty of
self: solitude is the richness of self' (May Sarton).
So how do we deal with that grief and loneliness
that suddenly surround us, and which we did
not choose?

I believe there is one answer, and that is friendship. Friendship with God and friendship with
others. Jesus knew loneliness in his life. He knew
the loneliness that could support and build him up.
We read in Luke 5.16 'Jesus went out to a lonely
place and there he prayed'. But later on in his life
we read 'My God, my God why have you forsaken
me?' (Matthew 27:46). He knew the loneliness of
death and separation. He was prepared for that
loneliness by spending more time with his Father
in prayer and through close and intimate friendship with his inner circle of friends. If Jesus often
went out to lonely places and prayed, knowing
he was going to face death, should we not seek
that same help in friendship with God and close
friends, having faced death?

Shortly after a friend died, his widow read these
words in *Everyday with Jesus* written by Selwyn
Hughes. 'It is now several years since I laid my
wife to rest, and I have been asking myself what
treasures I discovered in the darkness of my
own bereavement. One that immediately comes
to mind is a new discovery of God and the truths
contained in his word. I had walked with the Lord
for forty years before my wife was taken from me
by cancer, and I had thought my intimacy with the
Lord was about as good as it could ever be. I found,

however, that the death of my wife produced in me a degree of grief and sorrow that I had never thought possible. I had known for several months that my wife's condition meant that her death was imminent but I was not prepared for the shock wave that went over me when it actually took place.

'"The eternal God is your refuge, and underneath are the everlasting arms . . ." (Deuteronomy 33:27) is a verse that had always been a great favourite of mine, but now, since I have passed through the darkness of bereavement, it has taken on a dimension that is almost impossible for me to describe. Just as a precious diamond is best seen against a dark velvet background, so does the truth of God shine more beautifully when set against those black moments of life such as death and bereavement. The truth of God shines most beautifully at any time, but believe me, never more illustriously than when set against the darkness of a bitter and heart-rending experience.'4

But you don't have to bear the grey cloud of loneliness by yourself. At times it will seem to overwhelm you, but help is at hand through family or friends or the church or the community. With others around they will help you share that burden. It may never leave you completely, but at least the warmth of the sun in the coldness of the day, and the light of love in the darkness will both begin to shine. Gradually tomorrow will not seem so long and terrible and empty. Others are there to share life with you.

Human friendship can mean so much. We can receive it from others, and also offer it in a way that perhaps we had never thought possible. There will be friends who will listen, care, understand and accept. They will share the pain and the tears, the laughter and the hopes. It is a friendship that takes time, and demands that we put ourselves in the place of our friends and anticipate their needs; that knows when to speak and when to be quiet. But it is a friendship that will enrich in a beautiful way those who give and those who receive. Such a friendship can never take the place of the one who has died. It is not a pale substitute or consolation. It is a human, ongoing friendship that can be offered and received on equal terms. It goes some way to lessening the loneliness of an aching and bereaved heart.

In the next chapter we shall look at how the church both corporately and individually can minister to those who are bereaved.

A Bible Reading:

The Lord is my shepherd, I shall not be in
    want.
He makes me lie down in green pastures,
he leads me beside quiet waters,
he restores my soul.
He guides me in paths of righteousness
for his name's sake.
Even though I walk
through the valley of the shadow of death,
I will fear no evil, for you are with me;
your rod and your staff, they comfort me.

You prepare a table before me in the presence
    of my enemies.
You anoint my head with oil; my cup overflows.

Surely goodness and love will follow me all
the days of my life,
and I will dwell in the house of the Lord for
ever.

(Psalm 23)

A Prayer:

Almighty God, you raised our Lord Jesus
Christ from death and gave him glory,
that I might have hope: have mercy on me in
times of despair.
My life seems to have lost its meaning, and
my hope has become so faint. Renew my
faith; help me to honour you by believing
you are able to make all things new, through
Jesus Christ our Lord. Amen.[5]

6

Caring for the Bereaved

Ted met me in our church lounge. 'It's a happy release', he said. I had been just about to say how sorry I was to hear the news that his wife, Ethel, had died suddenly in the Day Centre of the hospital. I had known Ted and Ethel for some years. They had come week by week to our luncheon clubs. We had seen Ethel become progressively weaker, and I for one, could understand Ted's comment. All the pressures that he faced, day by day, in caring for her were now over. It was a release. But it was also a loss, and maybe in those first few hours and days, Ted hadn't yet realised how deep his loss would be.

Elizabeth Elliot, whose husband, Jim, died young at the hands of the Auca Indians in Equador expressed her feelings in these words: 'Silent, swift, implacable, the Scythe has swept by, and we are left . . . The mail comes, the phone rings, Wednesday gives place to Thursday, and this week to next week. You have to keep on getting up in the morning and comb your hair (for whom?), eating breakfast (remember to get out only one egg now), making the bed (who cares?)'[1]

How can we as individuals, members of a family, the church or the community, care for those who

are bereaved? I want to try to offer some help in
this chapter. I ought to add a word of explana-
tion before moving on. While we use the word
'bereaved' usually to mean losing someone in
death, the same feeling of loss can apply to other
kinds of loss in life. The loss of a job, the loss of
a home, the loss of friends when we may have
to move, the loss of children leaving home when
they get married or leave for college, the loss of
finance and status. These are all occasions of loss
or bereavement.

Often the sense of loss is not simple and
straightforward. Other factors can complicate the
picture. For example, the bereaved person may
be handicapped themselves and have been very
dependent upon the person who has died. They
may now face real financial worries, they may
have faced two or three family bereavements
in the past year. Troubles never seem to come
alone. There may have been tension and break-
up in the family and this grows worse now that
a loved one has died. There may be no one
who cares and understands. They feel dread-
fully deserted and alone. They may be carrying
a sense of guilt because they found it hard to
cope with the last few months of someone else's
illness. Maybe they had to be away from home
when a member of the family died. They find
it difficult to forgive themselves – especially if
they really didn't want to be around at the
time, as they were not sure how they would
be able to cope.

So against a variety of situations – all of which
are personal, and are marked out by loss, how
can we care?

The help of the individual friend

Such a person may be a member of the family, a fellow Christian or close friend. How best can we help?

May I share what I have personally found to be helpful? Make sure that immediately after the funeral you keep in touch either by phone or by just dropping in. Make sure that it would be welcome, and not an intrusion. You will know how to seek permission to offer this help and ministry. For example, ask, 'Do you mind if I just drop in when I'm passing to see if there is anything I can do to help?' Find out if there is any shopping to be done. Those who are bereaved don't feel like facing the crowds in shops just yet. They will plan to slip out for the few things they need either when it is dark or when they know they will meet very few people.

Be ready to talk over major issues – such as finances, what's best for the children, or whether to accept a friend's invitation to stay for a week. Be ready to hear what happened in the last days of the illness, as many times as the topic is raised. It is best for them to avoid making any major decisions before they are ready, and that may well be not before at least six months have passed.

Keep your eyes open and watch a person's body language. What you see will save you asking the obvious questions, and you will know how to respond. The downcast eyes and sad look will prevent you asking the question 'How are you feeling?' Physical contact matters. A compassionate hug says more than words can. Touch is what

is missing. Through our bodies we express our
feelings, and the kindly hug and the support-
ive arm will minister to the sense of loneliness,
or depression, darkness and indecision. Such an
action says 'I'm here with you', 'I care' and 'I
want to be with you and help'.

As we gain our friend's confidence, so they will
be able to share their sense of anger at God
or events, a sense of guilt that they feel there
is more they could have done, or the need for
forgiveness.

We have already mentioned that there are questions we need to avoid asking and traps we can so
easily fall into. It is so easy for us to feel that a
few weeks after the funeral they will be feeling
back to normal!! 'Are you feeling better now?' is
one question certainly not to ask.

As weeks turn into months and months into
years, the one thing that is more important and
helpful than anything else is friendship and love.
This will be especially welcome when evenings
seem long, or when difficult occasions such as fes-
tivals, anniversaries, birthdays and holidays come
along, and the gap and loss is most keenly felt.
For most people, even members of the family, life
returns to normal a few weeks after the funeral.
But not so for those who have lost a loved one. One
such friend wrote to me: 'I need close friends with
whom I can be totally natural, where I do not have
to pretend, who will accept me as I am, in my tears,
in deep grief, maybe in my anger. People who will
listen. I need physical contact – hugs!'

It is important that we don't leave those who
have been bereaved out of the social round and
the local party. They are now not sure of their

social identity and status. If they have lost their
husband or wife, how do they cope with 'other
couples'? Are they single again? They have to get
used to such words as 'widow' and 'widower'. How
important it is therefore, that we make everyone
feel they belong with us, and that we never allow
the bereaved to arrive or depart from events on
their own.

I am often taken back to the tender compassion
of the Lord Jesus for his mother and his commend-
ing her to the care of John (John 19: 25–27). Jesus
was asking John to take care of his own mother
– a most solemn charge and privilege – until that
relationship and trust was no longer needed or
possible. My own conviction is that bereavement is
made more bearable when friends can share that
quality of friendship with those who face personal
bereavement. Such support will ease the pain of
bereavement.

Help from the family

I know from more than thirty years in the pastoral
ministry that some families find it hard to cope,
and really have not faced up to the fact and reality of death themselves. The sister who might be
expected to support a lonely brother never phones
him up or drops him a card on special occasions.
No effort seems to be made to call or even to
invite him to stay for a few days. Parents can
leave their children to rebuild their lives after an
early bereavement, and appear amazingly blind
to the hurt a member of their own family is
experiencing. Other families, by contrast, have

drawn closer together, and are learning to face
the difficult times, helping each other.

Much of what I have written about the help of
friends will also apply to the help of the family.
The special help that parents and children can
share with each other at the time of a father
or mother's death will be covered when I write
especially about death and children.

The help of the church

A lot of help can be offered by members of the local
church, and I know that the visiting and care of
some members has been especially welcomed by
bereaved families not yet in regular contact with
the church. A visit from a member of the church
is usually welcomed. In some areas of the country
people just drop in. In other parts of the country,
and especially remote areas, it is best to phone
and fix a time to call, and then to arrive – in either
case – with a smile, and some means of identity,
because older people particularly will be cautious
whom they welcome into their homes. Don't hurry
your visit. Take time to allow the person to talk.
Be patient when they go over the same events and
stories a second or third time. Most likely they
have no one to talk to, and no one who is willing
to listen and understand.

Learning to listen

There is an art in becoming a good listener – and
that is what those who are bereaved long for. You
may find the following hints helpful. Accept people
as they are. Don't worry whether the sitting room

and the kitchen are in a mess, and the breakfast things are not washed up. Listen to what people are telling you, but also listen to where they may be hurting. Assure your host that what they tell you will be kept in confidence. Learn the art of asking the wise question. 'How do you feel?', 'Are you worried about money?' 'What did you have to eat yesterday?' 'Do you get many callers?' 'Does your daughter call often?' etc. You will learn to watch their 'body language' – how they are sitting, what they are doing with their hands and what they are looking at, and this will tell you how they are really feeling inside.

As we learn to listen to others, they will begin to share with us. Those we visit need to know that we are ready and willing to visit more often. Of course there is the danger of those we visit becoming wrongly dependent upon us, and urging us to call every day, and making demands upon us which we are not able to fulfil.

Most people, however, simply need the assurance that we really do care, and that we won't be just another person in the band of officials and friends who call just once at the time of the death. On-going, caring companionship is vitally important, and often it is the members of the local church who are able to offer that.

Writing in 'Coping with Crisis' Dr. Ruth Fowke tells us that 'most people are ashamed to admit their need of human help and companionship, yet it is essential for growth and health ... just as the body will slowly die if no food is taken in, so the personality shrivels and withers away if it is not continually nourished by regular contact

with other people.'[2] It is true that our sufficiency
spiritually is found in Christ. But it is also true
that our sufficiency socially is found with others.

Sometimes in our visits we shall be able to help
with some practical problem or need. We need to
learn the limits of the help that we are able to
give, and not to get ourselves into commitments
we are unable to fulfil, or promises we cannot
keep. A good dose of healthy realism in the face
of subtle emotional pressure will keep the visitor
from getting out of their depth.

I find it very helpful to leave a little card with
some scripture verses and a simple prayer that
expresses what our host cannot put into words
for themselves. As you grow in confidence yourself you will find it easier to suggest that the
visit ends with a simple prayer. The prayer may
include members of the family and close friends;
refer to some problem or situation that has been
talked about, ask for the Lord's peace and help,
and assure them of the Lord's care, protection and
blessing upon the house and home and those who
live there.

Sometimes there are circumstances that require
more than a simple personal prayer before we
leave. In some lives there are areas of deep pain
and hurt. There is resentment from the past that
has never been dealt with, areas where the need
for forgiveness has not been resolved, guilt that
has been eating away at a person inwardly. Just
as the body may need physical healing, so a life
sometimes needs inner healing in the area of the
spirit and emotions. The Lord is able to bring that
healing and wholeness to hurting lives, and it is
best to share that need with a minister or pastor,

or with a mature older Christian friend. If they are not able to help, they will probably know where such help can be found. Burdens that have been carried for months or years can be lifted and taken away by the risen Lord who died to take the burden of our sins and sorrows. As the psalmist puts it 'Cast your cares on the Lord and he will sustain you; he will never let the righteous fall'. (Psalm 55:22)

Sometimes the burden seems to be more than a heavy weight. It is more like a curse that binds us. Fortunately, we can be delivered from the 'curse' or 'bondage' that people have put upon us. The New Testament tells us that when the Lord Jesus died on the cross he became a curse for us, to set us free from the curse that sin and others had put upon us. (Galatians 3:13)

If I can use a very simple picture. Imagine someone who allowed their life to be bound with many strands of cotton. Jesus is like the person who comes along with a pair of sharp scissors and cuts all the strands one by one. It is possible for the person who was bound to feel the strands still. What they need to know is that the bonds have been broken and they can walk free in a way they have never known in their life.

Perhaps it is strange to include this in helping the bereaved, but death can be the time when we are very conscious of both the helps and the hurts of the past years, as we seek to build a fresh life.

Hindrances to recovery

There are, of course, attitudes and activities that don't help us as we seek to come to terms with

death. Pretending that it hasn't happened, and
living in denial, will only mean that all the
pain and sadness goes inside us, and poisons
our emotions and our bodies.

Equally unhelpful is the British disease of the **stiff
upper lip**. The refusal to cry, and the attempt to
bottle up our emotions. Again that won't help
because tears are the God-given means of expressing our emotions in the right and helpful way. It
is considered, by some, to be weak and unmanly
to cry. That isn't how God looks on tears.

In John, Chapter 11, we have the story of Jesus
being asked to visit a family he cared for. They
lived in the village of Bethany a couple of miles
outside the city of Jerusalem. Martha and Mary
sent Jesus the news that Lazarus, their brother,
was seriously ill. Then Jesus heard the news he
had died. When Jesus was able to visit the home
and the tomb where Lazarus had been laid, we
read – in the shortest verse in the Bible – 'Jesus
wept' (John 11:35). Yet we believe that Jesus was
the example of a perfect man. He wasn't being
weak, he was showing that it is part of being
perfectly human and manly to weep.

Another unhelpful reaction is to turn **towards
spiritualism** to seek help and comfort. I sometimes have strangers phone me up and ask for the
nearest spiritualist church. I find myself explaining that such approaches would not be helpful. An
increasing number of people, through a rise in a
belief in reincarnation, and through the spread
of the New Age, are trusting that there is a
life beyond this one and they are hoping they

will know the truth of this through spiritualism. Contact with the dead is forbidden in the Bible, and will lead us into serious delusion and unfulfilled hopes. It is much better for the Christian in their sadness to trust their loved one into the love and care of Jesus, rather than into the groundless promises and messages of the spiritualists.

Learning about ourselves

As we share with others in need, so we shall learn much about ourselves. As we help others come to terms with death so we shall have to come to terms with death for ourselves and for all those near and dear to us. We cannot be indifferent and detached towards death and at the same time helpful in our love and ministry to others.

For example, one reason why some doctors and nurses and others in the medical and caring professions cannot help a patient face death, is simply because the doctor or nurse concerned has not come to terms with their own death.

As we minister to others, we may find that they are ministering to us. Unrecognised pain from the past may surface in our lives, and we shall need to deal with that. Unprepared reactions about death may need to be examined, and unresolved anger towards others, and even towards God, may need to be confessed and released. We shall discover that all of us have limitations in caring for others. We shall be limited in our understanding, our time, our emotional capacity, our practical expertise to help. We may long to be able to help more than we can. Yet, even with the best will in the world, it is wise to know our limitations and to freely admit when we are unable to help or to understand.

There are other sources of help that should be mentioned here.

There are a number of **groups and organisations** that have been set up to help the bereaved. A short list of the best known is set out at the end of the book. They are only too ready and willing to help.

An increasing number of **local churches** are taking bereavement visiting and counselling seriously, and equipping suitable members of their congregations to care sensitively for the bereaved. We have one such group in our own church, and I know how much the regular visits to those who have been bereaved are appreciated.

Encourage the bereaved person to call on their **local G.P.** and share problems that they have with him or her. They will know whether a listening ear or some medical prescription is what is needed.

If there has been contact with a **nearby Hospice** at the time of the illness and death of a relative, you will find that the staff of the Hospice will be willing and able to help them in their hurt and grief following the funeral. The Hospice movement, as we shall discover in a later chapter, is committed to unhurried caring both for the dying, as well as the family of the dying. They have a marvellously loving and positive ministry, and will help them face their fears and panic about the future.

As well as organisations that are set up to help, there are also some **simple books** that many have found helpful to answer questions about different aspects of their experience. At the end of this book I mention just a few of them.

A Bible Reading:

Praise be to the God and Father of our Lord Jesus Christ, the Father of compassion and the God of all comfort, who comforts us in our troubles, so that we can comfort those in any trouble with the comfort we ourselves have received from God. For just as the sufferings of Christ flow over into our lives, so also through Christ our comfort overflows. If we are distressed, it is for your comfort and salvation; if we are comforted, it is for your comfort, which produces in you patient endurance of the same sufferings we suffer. And our hope for you is firm, because we know that just as you share in our sufferings, so also you share in our comfort.

(2 Corinthians 1 : 3–7)

A Prayer:

Heavenly Father, please send forth your love and mercy to all who are facing the bitterness of bereavement, and the loneliness of their homes. Give each one a real sense of your peace and your presence.

Help them to face each day with faith and courage, and increase their hope in the Lord Jesus, who overcame death and opened the gate of life for us all, through Jesus Christ, our Lord. Amen.

7

Children and Death

'Little boys under five years old are most at risk from drowning in the family swimming pool at home.' That is the official statistic, but each child's death brings lasting pain and terrible anguish to their family. I have had to take the funeral services of older children horrifically burned through playing on rubbish dumps, and setting themselves alight from petrol cans. Others have died following months in hospital and many operations. Sometimes, I have had to bury one twin that has not survived. We have personally known miscarriages, and the death of children at birth. Whatever the occasion, the death of a child in the family is a tragedy. The marks will remain for a lifetime with the parents and any brothers or sisters. So how can we best help both parents and children?

Death of a child

Some practical help.

It will be very natural and right for both parents, but especially the mother, to spend time with the body of the child if that is at all possible. She may

be able to care for the body, caress her son or
daughter and cry alone, and say the things that
she was hoping to say later.

A whole flood of fears and disappointed hopes
will arise. The parents have not only lost a child,
they have also lost the future. All the hopes of
school, success, marriage, shared holidays and
having grandchildren have been snatched away
from them.

We must not rush the discussion about the
funeral plans. Death has often been without war-
ning, and possibly neither parent has had to face
a death before, so they are quite unprepared, and
are not sure what to do. All the issues that we
have already discussed for the 'day of the funeral'
of an adult are raised for a child, and it all seems
so harsh and pointless. It may be especially important to allow favourite toys to be buried with the
child, and to be completely free to decide whether
the funeral should be a very quiet service with just
the immediate family, or whether it would be a
help to include friends and school friends. It will
be very important to include other children in our
plans, to avoid terms such as 'God wanted Robert,
and that is why God took him', and to know that
children need to face death and to grieve as much
as grown-ups, but they do so in their own way.

There are organisations around the country
specially set up to help grieving parents. One
such is 'The Compassionate Friends'. (See list at
the end of the book).

We must always allow parents time to grieve
after the loss of a child. It doesn't help that the
father usually has to return to work, leaving an
emptiness at home for his wife to cope with. It

doesn't help for well-meaning friends or family to suggest that in the fullness of time the couple will be able to have other children and so make up the loss. A child can never be 'replaced' by a new baby.

The death of a child is a very personal and traumatic experience. We were not even allowed to attend the 'disposal of the body' of our own son, such were the habits more than thirty years ago. While I hold in my heart the hope that our son has stolen a march on us and got to heaven first, while I know he has skipped the trials of teenage years, and the hassle of life here on earth, I also know that we have missed out on much joy and many experiences that we would have shared together, and through which we would have enriched each other's life.

The questions that arise

It is important to take time to plan the practical details of the funeral, the change around in the bedroom, and the ways in which we decide specially to remember a son or a daughter. It is even more important to take time to answer the questions that are bound to arise. Among the first reactions will be shock. We can't really believe that it has happened. This is plainly true when death is the result of an accident, but it is also true when the child has been sick for months or years. The actual event of dying, and the irreversible fact of death is still a shock, and we need time to come to terms with it both intellectually and emotionally. So the time we are able to spend with the body will be time in which the fact of death begins to sink into our awareness.

There may well be guilt. What did we do wrong? Did we leave the gate unguarded, or forget to take the pan off the cooker, or not take the bath plug out? There will be lots of 'if onlys' and it is important that both parents have time to bring the fear and sense of guilt out into the open. There may be little that we can say to reassure one another, but it is essential that we can express our fears and worries, and help to see them in a clearer light.

Allied to guilt will be anger. If guilt is our reaction towards ourselves, then anger will be our reaction towards someone else. It may be the local council, or the school authorities, or our local doctor, or most likely God. If he is loving and if he is powerful, then none of this should happen. The death of a child raises some very important questions that we must not silence or deny. It is not always easy to answer them. There are many times when it is much better for others to listen quietly and reply 'I don't know' rather than to give an answer that plainly is unhelpful.

What I do know is that God is big enough to take our anger, and not be angry back at us. Instead, as we explode our anger upon him, he meets us with his loving understanding, for he is the one person in the whole world who can take our hurting and wracked bodies in his loving arms and hold us.

Death will bring a sense of dark separation upon us from all that is going on in the world. Our lives have stopped for a while, yet everything else is going on just as if nothing has happened, and we want to shout at the world as it passes by, 'don't you know, don't you care that my child has just died?' It doesn't even help much when the lady down the road tells you that the same thing happened to her five years ago. It is 'me' who is hurting at this moment in time, and it is 'me' who is walking through the valley of the shadow.

It is the loving and sensitive note that helps. We don't want anything 'too blessed', for our faith is still earthbound, and we can't soar with the wings of faith yet. We have to face the empty cot, and the meaningless nursery, the specially made-ready bedroom, or for the older child their favourite books and toys. What shall we do with them? Do we keep them? Give them away, or what? Every decision seems to be a major one, and we are not in a position to have the emotional energy to think too clearly.

Later on, we shall begin to find the answer to the question. 'Why?' but for the time being we can only breathe the prayer 'Lord, please give us your help and grace to walk through this valley'. I have found that this is the kind of prayer that our Heavenly Father is ready to answer.

It is our faith that holds us fast in the event of a child's death. At the time, that faith may be dented and bruised, but later we shall come to the point where we are able to accept that we had our child for a short or longer period, and then our son or daughter went to be with the Lord for ever in the Father's house.

The death of a child may well bring other children face to face with death for the first time. Usually the death of an adult raises the same issues, and I want to turn now from the death of a child, to death for a child.

Children and death

The day I began this chapter, my newspaper contained an article headed 'To say goodbye is important for a child'. The author wrote these words: 'Jack is aged six. In his short life he has suffered the loss of a grandfather, a pet and a hero. He came to my father's funeral; we buried the hamster in the garden, and on Easter Monday he and I attended the mass memorial service to his hero – the Freddie Mercury Memorial Tribute concert at Wembley. He grieved; three deaths – but the one that affected him most was Mercury's.' Then the writer, John Carey, continues 'Children do experience the pain and bewilderment of loss and bereavement. They have to go through the process of grieving. They, too, need to say their goodbyes.

'As Elisabeth Kulber-Ross, the psychiatrist acknowledged to be one of the world's leading authorities on death, has said: "It is important that we raise our children teaching them that death is part of life. We have to teach not only adults but young children that we can express our feelings openly and unashamed".

'To be able, aged two, to comfort his granny at his grandad's funeral; to be involved, at four, in burying our hamster; to go to Wembley, at six, to sing along at Freddie's farewell – all these have helped him to come to terms with his loss. They have also helped him to understand ours . . . on

Easter Monday, Jack said goodbye to Freddie and in the process we all grew up.'[1]

John Carey is right. For too long we have shut children away from the fact of death. As a result, we have made it more difficult for them to grieve and share their feelings. Secondly, we have made it more difficult for them growing up, to face death as adults. Thirdly, we now live in a nation that is unwilling to put death, as a natural and normal fact of life, on to the agenda, and so we confirm the conspiracy of silence. But how? That is the question. Children respond to death in the family in different ways according to their age. For example, a child who is under five will often see death as temporary. They will feel insecure, abandoned and afraid. They are aware, if it is a Mum who has died, that there is no longer Mum around to prepare meals, play with them and tuck them up in bed at night. An older teenage child begins to see and understand death as an adult does, but the death comes at a time when they are battling with all the inner emotions of their teenage years, and having to live with the help or mockery of their peers at school. It comes at a time when they are afraid to show what they really feel deep inside, for fear that their friends will reject them, not understand them, or think they are soft.

While children will react in different ways depending upon their age, the circumstances of the death, and the child's relationship to the one who has died, there are four major reactions that children will experience. They are fear, guilt, anger and confusion. In fact the child's reaction to death is very similar in outline to the reactions of a parent to the death of a child. The ways in

which those reactions are expressed, however, will
be different.

Fear

For example, the child who discovers that death
released fear within them, will be frightened of
losing the other parent, and feel insecure. They
will fear that they themselves might die soon, they
are afraid of going to sleep in case they don't wake
up. They are anxious about being separated from
other members of the family, or unprotected, and
at the same time they are scared of sharing their
feelings with others in the family in case they are
not really understood.

Guilt

The guilt that haunts them is just as real. They
feel guilty, thinking that the person's death is a
punishment for their own bad behaviour so that
it is their fault. This is especially true if they have
ever wished the other person dead. They caused it!
They feel guilty that they are still alive, and the
other person dead. 'It is not fair', they irrationally
think. Especially if they accuse themselves of not
loving enough the one who has died.

Anger

Anger is the third reaction they have to face. They
feel that they have been abandoned by the death of
a mother or father, and now they are going to have
to cope with their life on their own without the
help that other children have. They feel rejected
and unimportant – why have they been left? They
feel powerless and the future looms ahead of them

as something that is frightening and big, and they believe they are not able to manage.

Confusion

All of this – the fear and guilt and anger – leaves them feeling confused. They are confused about their reactions, about what they can or should believe about God and the future and their faith. They are confused about their moods, and about how other people think about them, and expect them to think and behave.

It is plainly clear that those closest to the children need to spend time with them to allow and encourage these thoughts and feelings to come out. Having said that, we may find that the children will find it easiest to share their feelings with an 'outsider' so that they don't hurt Mum or Dad who they know are also battling with their own loss.

Don't be surprised if the children eat a lot to satisfy the inner pain, or, on the other hand, push their food away, saying repeatedly 'I don't feel hungry'. They will also feel physically tired and lacking energy and some may not want to go out with their friends socially. We as adults should be careful to allow them this 'space' to grieve in their own way, and not try to rush them along their journey of bereavement.

Each person will react in the way that is right for them. What we need to accept, however, is that no child should be shielded completely from the fact of death, and that every child will respond in some way that is right for their age and development.

So how do we, as grown-ups, cope in this situation that we have never faced before? Maybe it would help if I shared with you some guidelines for helping children who have experienced the death of someone they love. Here are ten suggestions:

Some guidelines to help

i. Don't be frightened to speak of 'death'. Any other word will give children a wrong impression. For example, what does a child think about 'sleep', 'gone to be with Jesus', 'God wanted them', 'they have gone to be in hospital and are not going to come back'. All these alternative phrases will give a wrong idea of God and Jesus and of what will happen to the child when they fall asleep or go to a hospital.

ii. Accept the fact that children have feelings, and experience numbness, anger, pain and emptiness in a similar way to adults. So to shut them out from death is to deny and suppress what and how they are feeling.

iii. Allow them to express their emotions. It is the suppression of feelings that is wrong. Let them cry, shout, scream or even sing so that God-given emotions can be released. After all, the grieving process is one that God has built into our lives, leading to recovery.

iv. It is wise to share the family bereavement with the school authorities and with activity leaders at church, Scouts, Brownies, etc., so that the leaders understand what they are going through and why the children are behaving as they are. A certain amount of regression may be taking place in their school work. This is quite usual, and if the teachers know why, they can take that into account.

v. There may be times when we, as adults, feel we cannot cope with our children's reactions. It is not a sign of weakness to ask for help from a Christian minister or a doctor, or someone concerned with child-guidance. Such a cry for help shows that we want to love and support our children all we can at this present time.

vi. Don't fall into the trap of telling a child that they are now the man or the woman of the house. Don't place responsibilities and expectations upon them that are too great and much too early for them. Again, and I write this from painful personal experience, don't tell anyone they are a replacement for a brother or sister who has died. I recall someone telling me when I was three 'If your brother had not died you would not have been born'. It took me more than forty years to be free from that feeling that I had to justify myself by what I did, and by what I was. Only when someone very helpfully prayed for me to be free from those words could I know that I was accepted for who I am personally, and for no other reason.

vii. It is not helpful to use stories or fairy tales to explain death to a child. It doesn't help to say that 'Daddy has gone away on a long journey', because then there is the hope that one day, Daddy will come back. It is better to use the Bible's pictures that we have already been thinking about, and

to tell a child as much as they want to know at
any one time.

viii. There will be questions that we are not able to
answer, and it doesn't matter if we have to say 'I
don't know'. The children want the truth in order
that they can trust us. If a child keeps on asking
for more and more, we may well have to explain
that God has told us only a little so far, but will
explain a lot more later on.

ix. It is helpful for children and grown-ups to have
the freedom to cry together and to share their own
feelings. If the children feel that we are holding
ourselves back, they will feel they should do the
same thing. Much better for a small child to discover us sitting on the sofa quietly crying and
allow them to come up, put their arms around
us and say 'Don't cry Mummy'. 'But I was just
crying for Daddy because I love him so, and miss
him so much, don't you?'

x. Above all, children do need a great deal of love
and assurance. They need to know that the loss of
one important relationship doesn't mean the loss
of other relationships. The greatest help that we
can give to children, as to adults who grieve, is
ourselves, our time, our love, and our hugs.

Children often want to ask the sort of question
that adults may not even think of asking. 'How do
you know that Grandpa is dead?' 'How do they dig
a grave?' 'What will happen to Grandpa?' 'Where
is he now?' 'How did he get to heaven?' 'If his
body is buried, how can he be in heaven?' Infinite
patience will be needed, the willingness to say

that we don't know; above all the assurance that whatever has happened, your love and care for the children with you remains as strong as ever.

We must never cease to reassure our children of our love. We shall need to say to them, again and again 'I love you'.

A Bible Reading:

He heals the broken-hearted and binds up their wounds. He determines the number of the stars and calls them each by name. Great is our Lord and mighty in power; his understanding has no limit.

(Psalm 147 : 3–5)

Jesus said: 'Let the little children come to me, and do not hinder them, for the kingdom of God belongs to such as these. I tell you the truth, anyone who will not receive the kingdom of God like a little child will never enter it.'

(Mark 10 : 14b–16)

A Prayer:

Heavenly Father, we don't understand why our child has died. We feel angry and empty about what has happened. Please help us to trust you in the darkness, and to find again your purpose and joy in life. We know that you understand how we feel because your only Son also died for us. We ask this in his Name. Amen.

8

So What can We Believe?

The journey through bereavement has been personal and painful. Having passed through the plains of illness, and the valley of death, we now stand at that place where time and eternity touch. We have been only too aware of time – it has dragged so slowly; but what can we believe about 'eternity' and of 'life' beyond the grave? What is the truth about the resurrection? Is there a heaven and if so what is it like? It is to those vital questions that we turn in this chapter and the next.

The first disciples faced exactly the same questions. When Mary, Salome and Mary Magdalene returned from the tomb in which Jesus had been laid, and said that the tomb was empty and that Jesus had risen, the disciples did not believe them. Luke tells us 'They did not believe the women, because their words seemed to them like nonsense' (Luke 24:11). To many people today the resurrection seems to be nonsense. Dead men don't rise!

The disciples however were not to remain in doubt for long. The Risen Jesus met with them. He met with some in the garden, with others on their journey. He spoke with them in the upper room and by the lakeside. He ate with them at

breakfast and at supper. He allowed them to
touch him. So compelling was the evidence that
they believed, and then devoted the rest of their
lives to telling others that Jesus had died for our
sins and had risen from the dead to give us life
and hope.

Although we can't meet Jesus in the same literal
and physical way that the disciples did, yet we can
still be sure that he is risen and alive. Spend a
little time reading the story in one of the four
Gospels and you will discover that there was an
earthquake, at which the soldiers guarding the
tomb fled, the stone was rolled away, and the
tomb was later found empty, the grave clothes
collapsed on top of themselves – just as if someone
had risen through the folded grave clothes – and
then Jesus appeared to his disciples. Sometimes
he appeared to small groups, but Paul tells us
(in 1 Corinthians 15:6) that he also appeared to a
crowd of 500 people at the same time, as well as
to himself on the Damascus Road.

The fact of the resurrection was told around
the country, the message spread to Greece, Rome
and Turkey, and the church began to grow. It
was founded on the reality of the resurrection.
Jesus was alive. That may seem fantastic and
even ridiculously impossible to modern minds, but
still it is true.

Just over sixty years ago, Frank Morrison was
a Fleet Street news reporter, who became weary
of hearing Christians claim that Jesus had risen
from the dead, so he set out to disprove the evidence and write a book to silence the church. He
read the accounts in the four Gospels – Matthew,
Mark, Luke and John, and he wrote a book entitled

'*Who Moved The Stone?*' in which contrary to his original plan, he set out convincingly the argument that Jesus *had* risen, and that therefore there is hope and life beyond the grave.[1]

When we face death – whether for ourselves or for someone we love – we need the certainty that death is not the end. Yet it is at those very times that we can be assailed by doubt and nagging uncertainty. The faith that once seemed so clear and simple, suddenly becomes full of question marks.

Don't worry if that happens to you, you may feel shaken, and think that your hold upon the Lord is weakening, but his hold on you will be just as sure and firm as it has ever been.

One man who helped many people feel and see the reality of the resurrection was the Revd. Peter Marshall. He was, at one time, the chaplain to the United States Senate. He was a compelling preacher. Speaking one Easter Day at the Westminster Presbyterian Church in Atlanta, he asked, 'What do I mean by resurrection?' Did he mean just the perpetuation of a dead man's ideas or influence? 'The resurrection is something we dare not water down by what we call "spiritualising" it. It must be so authentic that you and I can see it.

'... suddenly, at a given time between sunset and dawn ... there is a rustling as of the breath of God moving through a garden.

'A Man rises up from the cold stone slab where He had been laid.

'We must see Him as He walks to the threshold of the tomb, stands swaying for a moment on wounded feet and walks out into the dewy

garden, alive for evermore. We must be able
to see in mind's eye the discarded graveclothes
lying there, like a glove from which the hand has
been removed, the fingers of which still retain
the shape of the hand – lying there, collapsed a
little, slightly deflated, because there was between
the rolls of bandages a considerable weight of
spices . . .

'We must be able to *hear* it – catch a whiff of
the strange scents that must have drifted back to
the Man from that tomb of linen and bandages
of spices – myrrh and aloes – and close air and
blood . . .'[2]

One lady who listened to Peter Marshall on that
day in Atlanta found the fact of the resurrection
changed her life, gave her hope, and helped her
to meet with Jesus. She wrote: '. . . It was Easter
Sunday – a rainy, dismal day, thoroughly in tune
with my spirits. As my friend and I stood in line
at the church, I wondered why I was there. I had
just about lost any faith I had . . . My husband
"Sandy", a new 2nd Lieutenant in the Air Corps
stationed at Langley Field, had been killed in a
crash four months before. We had just one glorious
year together . . .

'By the time my friend and I got inside the
church, there were no seats left except the steps in
the balcony. I've never seen a church so crowded.
The service began. The music was lovely, and I felt
myself relaxing. Then the man in the pulpit began
to speak . . .

'How can I put into words what happened to me
in the next few minutes? It was as if the whole
crowd melted away, and there was the Lord and
I. As Dr. Marshall spoke of the resurrection, the

full meaning of it came into my heart for the first time . . .

'And when instead of a benediction, the vast congregation rose and stood silently while the choir, over a hundred strong, sang "There is No Death", I thought that I could not possibly stay in my skin and contain that moment of exultation.

'I walked away from the service on air. Out on the sidewalk my friend said, "What in the world has happened to you?" "Something wonderful, Virginia. The weight is gone. I'm all right now. I can go on living." But I said nothing more because just in case my new feeling of joy might be a passing emotion, I determined to give it a one year test before I told anyone in detail. Well, the peace that had crept into my aching heart and healed it that morning proved to be lasting. A year later, on Easter Sunday, I wrote Dr. Marshall thanking him for introducing me to the One who had brought joy back into my life . . .'[3]

This is the hope that my wife and I have for our little son who was born dead. He is not a pile of decomposed flesh and bones buried in some unmarked spot in Leeds, but a real person, eternally alive, whom we shall see again one day in heaven. He has by-passed life on earth, and has been taken directly to glory and heaven.

At the time it didn't seem like that. We were not able to say 'Good-bye' to him. Life was dark, heavy, purposeless, and most people didn't seem to understand how we felt. The hope of resurrection was a beacon of light that flickered at the end of a dark valley, but as we got nearer to the end of the valley, so the light shone more brightly.

For almost the last twenty years I have worked

in the parish of All Saints', Woodford Wells. The parish itself is in the London Borough of Redbridge and within the beautiful area of Epping Forest. At one end of the green, away from the church, stands a statue to a former Member of Parliament for the area, Sir Winston Churchill – the famous Prime Minister of the nation in time of war, as well as peace. Resurrection was the hope that sustained him. 'Only faith in a life after death, in a brighter world where dear ones meet again, only that, and the measured tramp of time can give consolation.'

Such a hope is based not only upon personal experience and evidence from the Bible, but also on simple logic. Does life make sense if we are only born to die? There is, in the heart of everyone, a sense of eternity. Does it make sense for God to make himself known to us in Jesus, through his birth, life and ministry, and then for Jesus to die in pain on the cross and be buried if there is no resurrection? What is the point? As St. Paul argued in 1 Corinthians 15, if there is no resurrection then there is no faith, there is no forgiveness, there is no future, there is no hope and we cannot trust anything that God has promised us.

What exactly is resurrection?

Different people mean different things when they speak about resurrection. For example:

The Jew speaks about the resurrection at the last day, but *not now*.

The Muslim believes that God raised Jesus from this world, but they also believe that Jesus never really died, and thus was not raised from the dead. He was only lifted into the presence of God.

The Buddhist believes in reincarnation, or karma. This hope in reincarnation is gaining acceptance in both east and west. More than one in four of the world's population believe it. Karma, simply, is the belief that a present life will be judged for good or evil and that the person will return to this world in a higher or lower form of life depending upon how they have lived. There is no forgiveness, no hope of heaven and no assurance about the future.

The Christian view is based upon the certainty that Jesus Christ was raised from the dead on the third day. The evidence for this is found in the promises of the Bible, the eye-witness accounts of the tomb from which the body was raised, the numerous appearances of the risen Lord to his disciples, the dramatic changes that took place in people's lives who met with Jesus after his resurrection, and the growth and testimony of the Christian church around the world, and down the ages of history until today. People in every corner of the earth today affirm that Jesus Christ is alive and risen from the dead. It is a universal truth, and a personal testimony.

In 1 Corinthians 15, Paul records this very firm foundation upon which the resurrection rests. Then he continues to explain the results of the resurrection for Christians then, and also for us today. If there is no resurrection, there is no faith, no forgiveness and no future. However, because Jesus is risen and alive we do have a faith, there is forgiveness, and we can be assured for the future both in this life and in the life to come.

But what sort of body will we have in the life to come? I have referred earlier to the accounts of the resurrection in the four Gospels. Dr. Luke, for example, mentions at least 21 times the Lord's risen body. Clearly, Jesus' body was a physical one, he was able to eat fish yet he also bore the marks of the crucifixion. But he was not limited by time or space. Together with the miracle of the resurrection we have the mystery of his body. St. Paul seeks to explain that mystery in 1 Corinthians 15:35–49. He argues that just as we have bodies suited to live on the earth, and fish are equipped to live in the sea, so we shall have bodies designed to live in heaven. 'The perishable will become the imperishable, and the mortal will become the immortal.' (1 Corinthians 15:53)

Dr. Billy Graham helps us to understand what happens to a Christian's body by using the illustration of a store that has to close for alterations. Later, the store re-opens with many changes and improvements. In the same way, a Christian moves out of his body until it has been renewed. Then at the general resurrection the spiritual man will move into his renewed body. As with Jesus there was a real difference and yet he was recognised most of the time, so with us. Our bodies will change but we shall surely know each other.

Burial or cremation?

The hope of a resurrection body raises the question whether people should be buried or cremated. The practice of cremation has increased greatly in the last thirty years. Is it right to cremate someone when they will be receiving a new body? I don't think it matters. Burial and cremation are both means of helping the body to decompose. While cremation solves the problem of needing to maintain the grave, it raises the important pastoral question of what do you do with the ashes if you wish to mark the place where they are interred. The present church laws don't help us. However, the truth of the matter is that whether slowly or more quickly, our earthly bodies will waste away. But we shall be given a resurrection body however our physical body has been dealt with.

Will we recognise one another in heaven?

Another question that is often asked is whether we shall recognise one another, and whether there will be close personal relationships in heaven just as there has been here on earth. Jesus taught that in heaven there will be neither marriage or giving in marriage (Mark 12:18–27). He went on to explain that life in heaven will be of a different quality from that here on earth, and that we shall be like the angels. But we shall know one another and greet the saints who have gone on ahead to glory.

What about animals and pets?

Others wonder whether their favourite pet will be with them in heaven. I think we have to say that while the Bible teaches us to care lovingly

for our animals and pets in this life, that they
are not the same as people. They have a body and
a mind and feelings, but they are not spiritual
creatures with a soul and unlike us they are
not made 'in the image of God'. When he made
man as the last act of creation, he breathed into
him and he became a living soul or a spiritual
being.

The fear of dying

For many people the fear of dying is greater
than the fear of death. Sir Malcolm Sargeant, a
famous conductor, when asked about death, said,
'I have no fear of death. I have enjoyed this life
but I believe death simply means a passing to a
better life.'

Making the journey is the problem. Knowing the
destination is the resurrection helps us face death
calmly and unafraid.

The communion of the saints

The resurrection to eternal life is not a solitary
affair, but the most marvellous invitation to join
the Communion of Saints. My own church is
dedicated to All Saints. As near as possible to
All Saints' Day (1 November) we sing:

> For all the saints who from their labours
>   rest,
> Who Thee by faith before the world confessed,
> Thy name, O Jesu, be for ever blest.
>   Alleluia!

O blest communion, fellowship divine!
We feebly struggle; they in glory shine,
Yet all are one in Thee, for all are Thine.
    Alleluia!

But lo, there breaks a yet more glorious day;
The saints triumphant rise in bright array:
The King of Glory passes on His way.
    Alleluia!

From earth's wide bounds, from ocean's
    farthest coast,
Through gates of pearl streams in the count-
    less host,
Singing to Father, Son, and Holy Ghost.
    Alleluia!

(Bishop W. Walsham How)

It is impossible to sing those verses without a feeling of hope and pride, and expectation. While death has shut the door on our earthly life, it has opened the door to our heavenly and risen life.

St. John, in the book of the Revelation, records his experience of looking through an open door into heaven and glimpsing something of what lay ahead, and the glory of the communion of saints. The more he looked, the more he saw. He tells us 'After this, I looked and there before me was a great multitude that no-one could number, from every tribe, people and language, standing before the throne and in front of the Lamb' (Revelation 7:9).

Such a scene is a great inspiration when we

feel lonely and isolated. Imagine the few people gathered in a small church for a communion service, but able to pray 'therefore with angels and archangels, and with all the company of heaven, we laud and magnify thy holy name'.

The same can be true for the lonely widow or widower finding that their worship and faith brings them closer to their partner. Separated for a short while, they will be reunited in heaven with them and with the communion of all the saints.

Will we have to wait?

One final question remains. Will there be a waiting time after we die before this all happens? Do I face purgatory or paradise? I believe the Bible teaches us to look forward to paradise.

Our Roman Catholic friends teach purgatory. This is not the idea of a second chance for those who have rejected God and his grace in this life, but it is God's loving work of purifying and perfecting those who are to be saved and yet are still bound in sin in some areas when they die. The idea is that by praying for those who have died, by offering Masses for them, their entry into heaven is hastened. But the Bible makes it much clearer than that, I believe.

Jesus promised the thief dying alongside him on the cross – 'Today, you will be with me in paradise' (Luke 23:43). Paradise is a picture of walking in the garden with the King. We shall walk in heaven with the King of kings. Paul looked forward to departing and being with Christ. He taught that 'in the twinkling of an eye' – and that is the smallest span of time – we would be changed. The imperfect would become the perfect. John said that when we see Jesus we shall be like him.

We need to be made perfect for heaven, but the Bible teaches that Jesus changes us in a moment; tradition teaches that there is a time of purification.

All this may seem like arguing over words but it is a real issue. Have you ever wondered what happens, if at the time of death, you are in such pain that you speak harshly to those caring for you? You are aware of sin and failure even at the approach of death. You wonder what you are going to do about that. We need to remember that Jesus has taken all our sins and so we continue to trust him and discover that his blood goes on making us clean and fit for heaven!

Molly had been ill with cancer for a few months. There was nothing more the doctors and nurses could do for her. Both she and her husband and their friends knew she was dying. We had prayed that Jesus would come and take her to be with him. The assurance of eternal life, the hope of resurrection, and the knowledge that she would go to be with Jesus was the most wonderful assurance and faith she could have. Of course, it didn't lessen the pain of separation, but Molly was ready to die.

George, on the other hand, seemed to be hanging on to life for a long time. He seemed to be so restless and unprepared. The family tiptoed around his bed, trying to pretend that he might even get better. For a number of reasons, unlike Molly and her husband, they were not yet ready to face death.

So how can we be ready to die? The heart of the matter rests on our understanding what the

New Testament teaches us about heaven and life
after death. While the Bible doesn't answer all
our questions, it does give answers to those that
really matter.

If we face those questions, we shall actually
begin to enjoy life and the future.

A Bible Reading:

Listen, I tell you a mystery: We will not all
sleep, but we will all be changed – in a flash,
in the twinkling of an eye, at the last trumpet.
For the trumpet will sound, the dead will be
raised imperishable, and we will be changed.
For the perishable must clothe itself with the
imperishable, and the mortal with immortality. When the perishable has been clothed
with the imperishable, and the mortal with
immortality, then the saying that is written
will come true: 'Death has been swallowed up
in victory.' 'Where, O death, is your victory?
Where, O death, is your sting?' The sting of
death is sin and the power of sin is the law.
But thanks be to God! He gives us the victory
through our Lord Jesus Christ. Therefore,
my dear brothers, stand firm. Let nothing
move you. Always give yourselves fully to
the work of the Lord, because you know that
your labour in the Lord is not in vain.

(1 Corinthians 15: 51–58)

A Prayer:

Heavenly Father, in your son Jesus Christ,
you have given us a true faith and a sure

hope. Strengthen this faith and hope in us all our days, that we may live as those who believe in the communion of saints, the forgiveness of sins, and the resurrection to eternal life; through your son Jesus Christ our Lord. Amen.[4]

9

Glimpses of Heaven

Where is heaven? What is it like? How do we get there? These are some of the questions that people have always asked about heaven and the future. They are questions that Jesus' disciples also asked. In reply Jesus told them about the promise of heaven.

The promise of heaven

'Do not let your hearts be troubled. Trust in God; trust also in me. In my Father's house are many rooms; if it were not so, I would have told you. I am going there to prepare a place for you. And if I go and prepare a place for you, I will come back and take you to be with me that you also may be where I am. You know the way to the place where I am going.' (John 14 : 1–4)

Of the 407 different mentions of heaven in the New International Version of the Bible this is perhaps the best known and most loved description that we have. Jesus tells his disciples – and us – five things about heaven.

Heaven is my Father's house

Heaven is where God is. God is Jesus's Father, and ours also. Heaven will be going home to Jesus. Heaven isn't the sky in which the birds fly and the stars shine. Heaven is not primarily outer space where the astronauts and cosmonauts have taken their spacecraft, and come back reporting that they didn't see God. But heaven, for Jesus and the Christian, means going to his Father's house.

Heaven has many rooms

So there will be room enough for all. We don't need to listen to the Jehovah's Witnesses who will tell us that only 144,000 people will be saved. There is room for everyone.

Heaven is not like Wembley Stadium and the FA cup final when you find that two clubs get a lot of tickets, some clubs get a few tickets, and most get none, and you have the hardest job in the world to get in. Wembley Stadium may have very restricted seating space, but heaven has many rooms.

Canon Scott Holland's following famous words are sometimes heard at a funeral service:

'Death is nothing at all. I have only slipped away into the next room. I am I and you are you. Whatever we were to each other, that we still are. Call me by my old familiar name, speak to me in the easy way which you always used.

Put no difference in your tone; wear no forced air of sorrow or solemnity. Laugh as we always laughed at the little jokes we enjoyed together. Play, smile, think of me, pray for

me. Let my name be ever the household word
it always was. Let it be spoken without an
effort, without the ghost of a shadow on it.

Life means all that it ever meant. It is
the same as it ever was; there is absolutely
unbroken continuity. What is death, but a
negligible accident? I am waiting for you,
for an interval, somewhere very near, just
around the corner. All is well.'[1]

These words provide a helpful picture, with one
exception. When we move from one room to
another in our house, the rooms are very similar.
But when we move from the room of our physical
life to the room of heaven we move from the
physical to the spiritual. Our bodies have been
left behind. It is our spirits or soul, that have
gone to be with Jesus, and are very much alive
in the rooms of our Father's House.

A place prepared in advance
Jesus tells us that the place has been prepared.
There are some lovely things that he has already
prepared for those who love him: a feast or banquet (Matthew 22.2), our inheritance (Matthew
25:34), personal blessings (1 Corinthians 2:9) and
also the rooms in heaven. We're expected and
we're welcome. Jesus has prepared the place for
us. He is ready for us.

A journey
There is a journey that we have to make. Many
Christians are not afraid of death, but they are
anxious about dying. David Watson once quoted

an American comedian (Woody Allen) who said
'I'm not afraid to die. I just don't want to be
there when it happens'. But the good news is
that Jesus has promised to come and take us on
that journey. Any new journey is a worry to many
people – whether the journey to school on the first
day, or to a new job. How will we know the way?
How do we know the way to heaven? We know how
helpful and reassuring it is when a friend promises
to come and call for us and take us on that journey.
That is exactly what Jesus promises here.

It is not unknown for a dying person who has
been asleep in their bed, suddenly to rise up and
reach out their hands and arms to welcome someone they can see. I believe that is Jesus coming for
them, and keeping his promise.

The destination

What's the destination? Jesus tells us that we
shall be where he is. There is going to be no waiting time to get to heaven. The thief on the cross
was told 'Today, you will be with me in paradise'.
Paul looked forward to 'departing and being with
Christ'. The same is true for every Christian.

Jesus has told his followers about his Father's
house – heaven – so that they will not be anxious.
We can be anxious for ourselves, and we can be
anxious about our loved ones. We want to know
where they are. Are they safe? Can we entrust
them safely to the Lord? Instead of being anxious,
Jesus calls his disciples to an attitude of trust.
'Trust in God. Trust also in me'. (John 14:1) We
shall be able to let go of loved ones, when we
are sure that they are safe in the keeping of the
Lord himself.

Tom came to me after one evening service at church. He was in his eighties, and his wife had died some seven or eight years before. He knew that heaven was not far off, and yet he longed to hear more about it before he went. I shared with him what I have just written and his heart was warmed and his faith encouraged. We all need that as we look forward to eternity; and we have the promises of Jesus to assure us.

As well as the promise of heaven, the New Testament tells us about the pictures of heaven, and the people who will be in heaven, and the passport – or the way to heaven. We will think about these topics one by one-

The pictures of heaven

There are pictures about heaven that will help us to think more clearly about eternity. It has been said that 'heaven is called a country that tells us about its greatness. It is called a city with its large numbers, and yet unlike any city that we will ever know in this world. It is a kingdom which speaks of God's rule and order. It is spoken of as paradise, a place full of wonder and delights'. All these pictures of heaven speak of the reality, wonder, glory and dazzling splendour of heaven. It is a place of beauty and delight, of harmony and love. It is a place of perfection and purity.

One of the fullest pictures of heaven – or rather the new heaven – is recorded for us in the apostle John's vision in Revelation, Chapter 21:1–8.

Then I saw a new heaven and a new earth, for the first heaven and the first earth had passed away, and there was no longer any sea. I saw the Holy City, the new Jerusalem, coming down out of heaven from God, prepared as a bride beautifully dressed for her husband. And I heard a loud voice from the throne saying 'Now the dwelling of God is with men, and he will live with them. They will be his people and God himself will be with them and be their God. He will wipe every tear from their eyes. There will be no more death or mourning or crying or pain, for the old order of things has passed away'. He who was seated on the throne said, 'I am making everything new!' Then he said, 'Write this down, for these words are trust-worthy and true'. He said to me: 'It is done. I am the Alpha and the Omega, the Beginning and the End. To him who is thirsty I will give to drink without cost from the spring of the water of life. He who overcomes will inherit all this, and I will be his God and he will be my son. But the cowardly, the unbelieving, the vile, the murderers, the sexually immoral, those who practise magic arts, the idolaters and all liars – their place will be in the fiery lake of burning sulphur. This is the second death'.

It really is worth reading the whole chapter, but even from these verses we can notice what will be there in heaven, and some things that will be absent.

What will not be in heaven
There will be *no sin*. There will be nothing that corrupts, or decays in heaven. There will be no sin

or curse. Nothing that is violent or destructive. There has been so much of that on earth. There will be nothing like that in heaven.

There will be *no separation,* and *no barriers.* We shall be with our Lord, and with our loved ones who have trusted Jesus, for ever. Some of the most difficult things in this life have been the partings – whether for a weekend, an overseas trip, the children leaving home, a period of illness, or worst of all – death. But heaven tells us that there will be no more partings.

There will be *no sadness* (v.4.) What a lovely picture of God gently wiping away every tear from our eyes. Joni Erikson, who while still a teenager broke her neck in a diving accident and has lived and written and painted from her wheelchair ever since, has written 'When I think of heaven, I think of a time when I will be welcomed home . . . The wrongs and injustices of earth will be righted. God will measure out our tears which he has kept in his bottle, and not a single one will go unnoticed. He who holds all reasons in his hand will give us the key that makes sense out of our most senseless sufferings. And that's only the beginning.'

There will be *no sorrow.* Life on earth has been marked out by sorrow and disappointment. There have been many times when we have cried inwardly, even if the tears have not flowed outwardly. There has been crying and mourning and weeping. But in heaven, there will be no more. Instead, there will be the joy of meeting loved ones again.

There will be *no suffering*. No emotional hurts and pains. No physical limitations deformity or disabilities. The aches and pains of life will be over.

Heaven is the place where we shall be with Jesus, and we and our loved ones will be set free from all that hurt us and gave pain – from sin and separation, from sadness and sorrow, and from suffering. Instead there will be much to please and satisfy.

What will be in heaven

We often get our ideas about heaven from our imagination, or from other people's pictures. Amongst the best known are John Bunyan's description of heaven in *Pilgrim's Progress*, John Milton's in *Paradise Regained*, and some of the symbolic pictures by William Blake. All these have much truth in them, but we are on safer ground when we are content to get our ideas of heaven from what God has shown us in the Bible.

Many people think that we shall be spending our time in endless, dull, repetitive worship. Nothing could be further from the truth. We shall be caught up in worship that will be vibrant and exciting, satisfying every part of us. Even the best worship here on earth will be a pale reflection of the worship in heaven. It will be as different as the most splendid banquet with friends would be from eating cold fish and chips on your own on a dull and wet Saturday evening.

But worship is not the only activity in heaven. There will be work and rest. We are told we shall serve or minister to the Lord himself. We don't know what each will be doing, but if we bear

in mind that the God we serve in heaven is
the one who has produced endless varieties of
created things here on earth, then surely heaven
must be even more splendid. The picture that the
book of the Revelation paints is one of purity and
great beauty, of grand scale and intricate detail. Of
order and freedom. A city of gold that will never be
tarnished. A community of people from every part
of the world, and every period of history in which
there is no problem of language, and no division in
relationships. There will be recognition, and welcome. We shall feel that at last we have arrived,
and become what God intended us to be ever since
the day he first made man.

The people of heaven

Not everyone will be there. The saints down the
ages will be there. The multitude of angels – God's
faithful messengers who have been concerned
with our welfare while on earth will be there.
Jesus will be there. God will be there. But as we
read in the book of the Revelation 'the cowardly,
the unbelieving, the vile, the murderers, the sexually immoral, those who practice magic arts, the
idolaters, and liars will not be there'. Their place
will be the fiery lake of burning sulphur. We are
also told that 'nothing impure will ever enter it,
nor will anyone who does what is shameful or
deceitful, but only those whose names are written
in the Lamb's book of life'. (Revelation 21:8,27) For
many people those verses – and the truths they
express – raise very real problems, and I want
to try to answer them, so that we are personally
reassured about 'going home'.

To help us understand, let me first recount a very ordinary event that happened to my wife and myself one afternoon. We had been out for a couple of hours, when we got back we went upstairs to our bedroom and discovered we had been burgled. They had taken all Stephanie's jewellery, including her engagement ring, and also other special gifts from her mother. We experienced, like everyone else to whom this happens, the feeling that that which is sacred and special had been defiled by someone's sin and greed. If that is our feeling over personal jewellery being stolen, how much greater must be God's feeling that heaven must not be profaned.

It is hard for most people to believe that there is both a heaven, where God is, and a hell, where God is not. It is equally hard for most people I meet at funerals to believe that living a good life is not a good enough basis upon which God accepts us into heaven. We forget that everyone will appear before the judgement seat of Christ (2 Corinthian's 5:10). The writer to the Hebrews reminds us that it is given unto men to die once and after that is judgement. (Hebrews 9:27)

We shall be judged according to the lives we have lived, the works we have done and the words we have spoken. It is an awful prospect for most of us. But the one who will act as our judge is the Lord Jesus Christ. The Father has appointed Jesus as the Judge (John 5:22).

Jesus will announce that we have all sinned and fallen short of God's standards and God's glory. But then he will add that he died on the cross on the first Good Friday for all who are sinners,

and that he forgives all who have sinned, and
confessed, and turned from their sin. Heaven is
for all forgiven sinners. Where our sin is great,
God's love and grace is greater.

Let me tell you of a wedding I shall never forget. Two of our Bible class leaders were getting
married. The service had finished. We were in
the vestry to sign the registers. The pen that
was prepared didn't appear to write. So I opened
the desk drawer to get the ink. We completed
the signing without trouble, and then I screwed
back the lid, and began to put the ink bottle
away. Unfortunately, the top was not securely
fixed and just when I thought all was well, the
bottle dropped a few inches on to the table, and
the ink began to spill on to the glass top, and from
the glass top on to the bride's dress as she sat at
the desk!!

I was horrified. What could I do? I had ruined
their day. A resourceful mother-in-law pinned the
full skirt of the bride's dress over, the unflappable
bride went down the aisle with her flowers held
down slightly, and everyone acted as if nothing
had happened. Fortunately, later the dress was
plunged into milk and the stains removed. But
I shall always recall my mistake and fault, but
even more the love and forgiveness I received
that covered – literally – my sin. There was
nothing else I could do. Someone else had to
deal with my sin for me. That is exactly what
Jesus did for us, when he died on the cross
that my sin might be forgiven, and when he
rose again to assure me of his cleansing. As
the hymn *There is a Green Hill far Away,* puts
it:

'There was no other good enough to pay the
price of sin,
He only could unlock the gate of Heaven
and let us in.'

When we trust Jesus for our forgiveness, and our
names are written in the Lamb's book of life, then
we have the right and privilege to enter heaven
when we die. Of that we must be certain. As John
records in his gospel 'I tell you the truth, whoever
hears my word and believes him who sent me
has eternal life and will not be condemned; he
has crossed over from death to life. (John 5:24)
We shall not avoid the day of judgement, but we
shall not be condemned in it. Rather we shall be
welcomed for ever into the very presence of God
in the glory of heaven.

That hope of heaven is fine for the committed
Christian, but what about many who are not sure.
Like the lady who asked me recently 'My father
was not a Christian when he died, what will happen to him?' Or the newly married teacher in my
congregation who told me that many teenagers in
her school were worried about hell. It is the same
question that arises in the mind of a surviving
spouse, who, in the aftermath of bereavement
comes back to a personal Christian faith, only
to find that she is now worrying about what has
happened to her husband who died without any
firm personal faith in God. What will happen?

May I share what I have shared with them. It
is not only their question. It was mine also. I well
remember my own father, who died more than
25 years ago, telling me what he had witnessed
in the trenches of the River Somme in the first

world war. Those scenes made it impossible for him to believe in God. As an enthusiastic young Christian student I had tried to tell my dad about Jesus. I don't know whether he believed or not when he died. But I do know that just before he died, he gave our daughter a picture of Holman Hunt's *Light of the World* with the words written on the back 'One day daddy will tell you what this means'. Many of us agonise over just such a situation.

First, we need to acknowledge that God is the judge and we can be assured that the judge of all the earth will do right. (Genesis 18:25)

Secondly, we know that the judge will ask how we have responded to the truth that we have received and understood. (That's a summary of Paul's argument in Romans Chapter 2). That can vary in every situation. We know that God's judgement will be fair and loving and good.

God's concern is that all should repent and come to the knowledge of the truth and that none should perish. To that end God has barred the way to hell, and pointed the way to heaven, with the message of the Bible, the ministry of Jesus through his life and death, and the mission of the church throughout history – to tell people the way to heaven. God intends that we all have our passports in order and ready to present when we set out for heaven and our Father's home.

The passport to heaven

It was Thomas, one of the twelve disciples, who asked Jesus the way to the Father's house. 'Lord,

we don't know where you are going, so how can we
know the way?' (John 14.5)

To that fundamental question Jesus answered
'I am the way and the truth and the life. No-one
comes to the Father except through me'. (John
14:6) Jesus had previously referred to himself as
the gate to life that we need to discover. 'I am the
gate for the sheep' (John 10:7), and again: 'Enter
through the narrow gate. For wide is the gate and
broad is the road that leads to destruction, and
many enter through it. But small is the gate and
narrow the road that leads to life, and only a few
find it'. (Matthew 7:13–14)

Those words of Jesus from Matthew always
remind me of a party our children were invited
to in Sheffield when they were very young.

They had some school friends who lived in a
wonderfully large house on the edge of the city.
The gardens were vast, and to enter the house, for
us, was like entering another world. Deep carpets,
rich paintings and displays on the walls. Furniture
and possessions the like of which we had not seen
before. They had a great time. But to get to the house
we had to go along a narrow lane and then enter
through quite a small gateway. It seemed the only
way in. It always speaks to me of the narrow road of
trusting and following Jesus, and going through the
gateway of admitting our need, humbling ourselves
and starting to follow Jesus.

Entering through such a gateway, said Jesus, is
essential for everyone. He had been asked 'Who
is the greatest in the kingdom of heaven?' He
replied 'I tell you the truth, unless you change
and become like little children, you will never
enter the kingdom of heaven. Therefore, whoever

humbles himself like this child is the greatest in the kingdom of heaven'. (Matthew 18:1–5) Gateways can be both exciting and sad places. The departure lounge of any airport in the world will contain friends who are seeing loved ones leave for another part of the world. For them, that gateway is a sad place. So for us who remain here on earth the gateway of death is a sad place. For those about to travel, there is a mixture of fear and joy. Have I got my ticket, my luggage, and above all, have I got my passport and is it in order? Without that passport there will be no departure and no entry. But when our names are written in the Lamb's Book of Life, we can look forward to heaven trusting not in what we are or have done, but trusting only in Jesus.

With our passports in order, people on this side of the gate will wave 'goodbye' and say, 'There he goes'. But others – at the end of the journey, waiting to welcome us into heaven and eternity will be saying 'Here he comes. Welcome into the presence of the Lord and to your Father's house'.

Do you have your passport into heaven and the Father's House in order? Is it stamped with the Saviour's name?

A Bible Reading:

After this I looked, and there before me was a door standing open in heaven. And the voice I had first heard speaking to me like a trumpet said, 'Come up here, and I will show you what must take place after this.' At once I was in the Spirit and there before me was a throne in heaven with someone sitting on it.

(Revelation 4:1,2)

Then I looked and heard the voice of many angels, numbering thousands upon thousands, and ten thousand times ten thousand. They encircled the throne and the living creatures and the elders. In a loud voice they sang: 'Worthy is the Lamb, who was slain, to receive power and wealth and wisdom and strength and honour and glory and praise!'

(Revelation 5:11,12)

A Promise to Claim:
Jesus said:

'I tell you the truth, whoever hears my word and believes him who sent me has eternal life and will not be condemned; he has crossed over from death to life.'

(John 5:24)

A Prayer:

Lord Jesus, thank you that the door into heaven and your presence is open. Thank you that you died on the cross for sinners, and rose again to give us life. I want to be sure that I have eternal life and will spend eternity with you, and those I love. Please forgive the many times when I have lived my life without you. I admit my need of you each day. Help me to follow you, love you, and know you. Give me the gift of your Holy Spirit so that you are real to me and living with me from this day on. For Jesus' sake. Amen.

10

Making a Fresh Start

D eath is loss. But death can also be gain to
those left behind. We are aware that we
feel empty and something has died inside us. It
is almost impossible to believe that we can live
and grow again as a person. The dark clouds of
depression and loneliness hang over us, threat-
ening never to move away, and we find it hard to
believe that there is a sun of hope shining behind
them. We wonder if it will ever be possible to
make a fresh start in life and within ourselves.
So as we try to face the future we need to be
very practical.

Some practical issues

Don't rush into important decisions. If you are
left alone in the house, the children may well
ask whether you will move nearer to them. Will
you start work again? Will you stop work? Will
you go on a spending spree; or make far-reaching
financial decisions? If you are mourning the death
of a child or a young person will you at once decide
to have another baby; or adopt or foster? In the
weeks after the funeral your feelings still change
a great deal. It is wise to delay any major decisions

until you have had time to think them through, and talk them over with friends and family.

You will need to clear out wardrobes and cupboards, tidy out a bedroom and decide what to do with toys, favourite clothes and possessions. The guiding rule seems to be 'Do it when you feel you can. Do it little by little.' Inevitably, you will start a job, and then find that it is too much. You come across some favourite photographs, stop what you intended to do, sit on the bed and look and think, remember and cry.

What will be important is to decide that there will be some things that you intend to keep. There will be others that must go to 'a good cause', or that you want to pass on to other people.

You may decide, in due course, to re-decorate a room or to re-arrange some photographs.

During all this time, you will be learning the need to fix a different pattern to the day. For example, the time you get up, the routine that gives shape to the day, when you do the shopping, how you plan to cook and eat, how you plan to fill those times that will be especially difficult. We need to remember that life will never be the same. However well we make a new start, we shall live with the pain of loss for the rest of our lives. That loss may become a healed scar in time, while for some it stays more like a gaping wound that is allowed to fester. It is probably a pain that we will in fact never want to lose completely; Jeanne Scheresky has expressed this feeling beautifully in her poem 'Promise of Springtime'.

A bare oak tree is a symbol of a
life that is left alone, stripped of all
that is good and worthwhile and dear –
lonely, empty, and dead.
As the oak tree blooms anew each spring, so
I have faith that God will someday bring
springtime to my heart and life again.
But I never want to be so happy that I
forget these long, dark, painful days,
when I proved God's promises are true.[1]

There will be times when you think that you
have got on top of your fears and feelings, then
suddenly, out of the blue, you get knocked down
again. There will be other times when courage is
strong, and you can face the pain with greater
confidence. Behind all the practical issues and
decisions will be your hope and your faith and
how you view the future.

Grounds for hope

On the fifth anniversary of the day when Terry
Waite was captured in Beirut and then held hos-
tage, he visited his former boss – The Archbishop
of Canterbury – at Lambeth Palace. At the time of
Terry's captivity none of his family knew whether
he was alive or dead. Only after he was released
did the world hear of the traumas he went through
and the trials – even a mock execution that he
faced, and the fact that he was kept blindfolded
and handcuffed in a foetal position for months on
end. How could he have hope in that situation?
On that anniversary, five years later, Terry Waite
issued a statement that included these words.

'The assurance that I wasn't alone was based on a faith rooted in the knowledge of the greatness of God, which, while suffering is being endured, is not always easy to recognise or remember but on reflection is deeply sustaining. It may take a long time to recognise how deeply sustaining that faith is. Suffering is not made easier by the Christian faith but faith makes it bearable and possible for it to be transformed into something creative for oneself and other people. To the lonely and isolated I have the message of hope that God does care and support us.'

Another man who walked that path was Prebendary Webb Peploe, who in his day was a noted preacher and Christian leader. As a young married man Webb Peploe took his young family to the seaside for a holiday, and one of his little children was drowned. He came back to London devastated with grief. In his study one day he poured out his grief before God. He pleaded that God would make his grace sufficient for him in his deep need. He found no help or comfort. His desolation and guilt was as strong as ever. Then through his tears, he looked up at a favourite text from the Bible that hung on his study wall. 'My grace is sufficient for thee'. (2 Corinthians 12:9) For the first time he noticed that the 'IS' was picked out in large letters. He suddenly realised that he had been asking God to make his grace enough to help with his loss, when all the time God had been telling him that it IS sufficient. He had to receive that help and grace by faith. His sense of loss was no less, but he now found that the comfort and love of God flooded his heart and he had a peace he had not known before.

I know no other lasting source of help and

comfort in death than that which is founded on our Christian faith. Thousands of Christians around the world would give the same testimony.

For example, a wife and mother wrote these words:

'Somebody I love has died'

Somebody I love has died;
they won't ever
laugh, shout,
joke, cry,
kiss, cuddle,
tease, torment,
tell me off
again.
There's an empty place at the table,
an empty space in my heart.
It's tough, Lord,
but then ... you know.
Somebody you loved died too.

Wendy Green.[2]

Such faith will help us hang on in the darkness, even though we cannot see the light. A Jewish prisoner once wrote on a prison wall in Cologne these words:

I believe in the sun even when it is not
shining.
I believe in love even when I cannot feel it.
I believe in God, even when he is silent.

Such a faith will cause us to turn again and again

to the Lord in faith and hope. A young man lost his fiancée in a drowning accident only days before their wedding, and immediately after her funeral wrote these words:

What a friend we have in Jesus,
All our sins and griefs to bear!
What a privilege to carry
Everything to God in prayer!

O what peace we often forfeit,
O what needless pain we bear
All because we do not carry
Everything to God in prayer.
                              Joseph Scriven (1820–86)

Those words are a remarkable testimony that not everyone would be able to echo. Whatever the circumstances of our loss, we shall probably find ourselves facing a number of searching questions.

Frequent questions

The most frequent question will be 'Why?' Why has this happened to them, and why has this happened to me, or to us? Why did that mother die so young? Why did we lose our only son, when we had prayed so long to have a family? Why did my husband have to suffer so long and painful an illness? Why couldn't the Lord have just taken him? What was the point of all that suffering? So the questions could continue. I asked the same questions when our son didn't live. Why the waste? Why the pregnancy that led to death and not to life? So long as I continued to ask those questions in the early days, I received no answers. Only when I began to ask that the Lord would give us his grace to continue the journey through the valley of the shadow of death did I know the Lord's presence and hear his voice. Much later, I began to understand and see there was gain in death for us, both through the daughter we adopted, as well as the understanding I was able to offer in my ministry to others. Thousands before and after us will ask the same questions. We may not get the same answers, but if we listen to the voice of the Lord, we shall hear his reply at the right time.

Another question is 'How can I find God in times of crisis? He so often seems to be more remote than ever! You will not be alone in thinking like this. Many do. There are three things that we can do that will help.

Trust God in the darkness
I wonder if you know the lovely piece of writing called 'Footprints in the Sand'?

One night a man had a dream. He dreamed he was walking along the beach with the Lord. Across the sky flashed scenes from his life. For each scene, he noticed two sets of footprints in the sand; one belonging to him and the other to the Lord. When the last scene of his life flashed before him, he looked back at the footprints in the sand. He noticed that many times along the path of his life there was only one set of prints.

He also noticed that it happened at the very lowest and saddest times in his life. This really bothered him and he questioned the Lord about it.

'Lord, you said that once I decided to follow you, you'd walk with me all the way. But I have noticed that during the most troublesome times in my life there is only one set of footprints. I don't understand why when I needed you most you would leave me'. The Lord replied, 'My precious, precious child. I love you and I would never leave you. During your times of trial and suffering, when you see only one set of footprints in the sand it was then that **I carried you**.' (Author unknown).

We need also to understand that at times like this God is nearer than we realise. There was the time when Jesus seemed to be asleep, with the disciples in peril on the Lake of Galilee, yet he was there to deal with the fear, and the storm. So often he is nearer than we expect. When we cry out to him, he is there.

Praise God
I well remember the morning the news of the North Sea oil disaster came through when 160 men were killed at the Piper Alpha platform. We were at a meeting in Canterbury, with some hundreds of Christians from around the world.

Some of the African Christians present had faced the brutal martydom of some of their own family and friends. The circumstances were very different, but the horror and pain were similar. In

those tragic situations our African brothers and
sisters would start to praise the Lord. That perhaps sounds strange to us. Yet as they magnified
the Lord that day in Canterbury, so their praise
began to put the horror and the tragedy and loss
into some kind of perspective.

Seek him.
So, when God seems so remote, we must seek him.
The Psalms often tell us that the Lord is found by
those who seek him. As we draw near to him, so
he draws near to us. (James 4:8)

Ready to die?

Are we ready for death ourselves? That may
seem a very odd question to raise. Our own death
may in fact be the very event that we long for. It
will save us the pain of our loss, and the emptiness
of the years that seem to stretch unendingly ahead
of us. Death would be a happy release. I don't
mean the question in that way. Death is not
only a happy release, but it is the coming into
the presence of the Lord and we may suddenly
realise that we are not yet ready to die. There
would be things in our lives that we would want
to put right. There are members of our families
that we are not ready to leave. The thought of
death or suicide may be natural, but it is selfish
as well as against God's plans for our lives. He is
the giver of life and only he can take it away.

A very different question that will probably occur
to those who face bereavement in the midst of life
is whether they should consider **remarriage**. For

some they would never wish to marry again. Their experience of marriage was either so good they would fear that a second would be second best, or their experience of marriage was so painful, they would not wish to get married again. For others, both husband and wife have talked over this possibility knowing that one of them would die first. They have released each other from the fear of disloyalty, and the guilt of betrayal that otherwise they might have had to deal with. This surely is a question about which we must not hurry an answer and a matter in which we must not be bound by the suggestions and expectations of others. The answer for some will be, 'I never would wish to marry again'. Others will need the love and companionship of a second life partner, knowing that one of them will face the pain of bereavement again as they commit themselves to the joy of marriage and companionship.

As we move on from the point where time and eternity touch, and where the physical and the spiritual merge, so we will find that our sense of what is important begins to change. What the changes might be were highlighted in a recent survey among elderly people. Fifty people over the age of ninety-five were asked the question 'If you could live your life over again, what would you do differently?' A variety of answers were given, but three answers constantly re-emerged in the study. They were these:

i.   I would reflect more.

ii. I would risk more.

iii. I would do more things that would live on after
I am dead.[3]

So there is, on reflection, a growing awareness
that there is not only life after death for those
who have gone on ahead, but there is also life after
death for those who are left, and who have to continue to make the journey through bereavement to
a fresh start.

At this stage in the journey some important pastoral issues begin to emerge, and with consideration
of these we must draw our journey to a close.

Pastoral issues

Our own spiritual life

We have been so occupied in giving out, during
the illness and death of our loved one, that we
haven't realised how spiritually empty and dry
we have ourselves become. Others have done the
praying for us, and fed us with thoughts and Bible
verses. Now is the time to take stock, and gently
resume or form the habit of reading a part of the
Bible each day. You will have to choose the time
and place that is best for you. It may be first
thing in the morning, or during a quiet period in
the morning or evening. Set aside ten to fifteen
minutes to begin with – you will probably find that
the length of time expands as you find this activity
more and more essential. There are a number of
Bible reading helps such as the various notes
from Scripture Union, CWR (Crusade for World
Revival) and the Bible Reading Fellowship. Your
local church or Christian bookshop will tell you
what is available.

You may wish to read those passages of the Bible that are specially linked with the theme of death, heaven, hope and encouragement. Twelve of the best loved passages are: Psalm 23; Psalm 46; Ecclesiastes 3:1–6; Isaiah 43:1–7; Jeremiah 29:10–11; John 11:17–44; John 14:1–6; 1 Corinthians 15; 2 Corinthians 1:1–11; 2 Corinthians, 4 & 5; Revelation 7:9–17 and Revelation 21:1–5.

You will find that the Bible is food to your hungry soul, and light to your bewildered mind. As you journey through your sadness God's word will be a lamp to your feet and a light to your path. (Psalm 119:105)

It was C.S. Lewis in his book *A Grief Observed* who saw this journey and he wrote: 'Bereavement is an integral part of our experience of love. It follows marriage as normally as marriage follows courtship, or as autumn follows summer. It is not a truncation of the process, but one of its phases: not the interruption of the dance but its next figure.'[4] Thus an inevitable part of the journey will take most people through **old age**. We may well fear growing old with its failures and frailty and loneliness. Some will try to ignore it, and shut old age out of their minds and away from their responsibility. But the Bible teaches us to think positively about growing old. It is concerned to uphold the cause of the widow (Psalm 68:5), and it promises us that we shall still bring forth fruit in old age (Psalm 92:14).

Some cultures and traditions honour old age. The western world tends to shut it away. We may fear to become a nuisance and a burden to others. The death of a partner only serves to increase that fear and worry. It is not my purpose to deal with

the whole subject of growing old. Other books have
helpfully pointed out that 'The best is yet to be'.
They take a very positive attitude to growing old.
I only want to recognise the problem and concern
that may lay ahead for some, and urge us to
plan for our old age now while we are fit and
able to do so.

Learning to love again

Luci Shaw in her story of her husband's death
tells us of her feelings, and when she began to
realise she was able to love again. She writes:
'I'm glad that my single state is the result of
death, not divorce, which carries with it a weight
of bitterness and anger and psychic pain. My separation from Harold is clean-cut, with no breaks, no
regrets or remorse about unfaithfulness or disloyalty or neglect. I know he loved me wholly, as I
loved him.' Later she writes 'I think I am reaching
the point where I no longer need or expect all the
love and care to come in my direction; I want to
start giving it to others; to be free to both receive
and give.'[5]

The new shoots of giving and loving will probably spring up among the friends and family we
have always known. But new areas of activity,
and new interests will also begin to appear. The
course of study we had always intended to take,
the interest we had often wanted to develop will
now begin to find a place in our lives. The pattern
will be different for every person, depending upon
their circumstances and their personality and
their nature. A fresh start is possible for each
person who is willing to think and act positively
and bravely about the future. There is loss in

death, but we can begin to discover that growth
is also possible.

Growth through death

The truth that there can be growth through death
hit me forcefully as I read again St. John's Gospel
in preparation for our Good Friday and Easter Day
services last year. I realised that the first half
of the Gospel was about life. Then I discovered
that from chapter 10 onwards Jesus was talking
about death, and especially his death. He told his
disciples that as the Good Shepherd he willingly
laid down his life for the sheep. He shared the
pain and tears of death with the family of Martha
and Mary and Lazarus (chapter 11). The woman
(probably another Mary) came to anoint his feet
and body in preparation for his burial (chapter
12). Jesus kept the Passover, the Last Supper,
and he prepared his disciples for his death. He
went on to tell them about his departure, and the
preparation of the many rooms in his Father's
House. Then he prepared himself for his own
betrayal, suffering and death and ends with the
hope of the resurrection.

The death and resurrection of Jesus are unique
and cannot be repeated. But the blessing that
flows from his death is both universal and personal. We can face death because he had already
faced it and taken that journey through bereavement. Although his death is very special, yet the
truth that there can be growth through death need
not be unique.

We may not notice at once the tiny signs of
growth and gain. It may even seem to be heart-
less and disloyal to suggest that there can be gain

and hope and a fresh start in this life. But as we
allow the God-given processes of bereavement to
work themselves through, as our faith and hope
grow, as we know the love and support of family
and friends, so we shall begin to rebuild our life
and continue the journey through bereavement
and out from the shadows of the valley into the
warmer sunlight of the future.

All the way through this book I have tried to
take the fear out of death, and the mystery out
of dying. A right attitude to death will bring us
to a right attitude to life, and a right attitude to
ourselves will bring us to a right attitude to God
and to the Lord Jesus.

When these things are true, then we can look
upon death as 'going home' to be with those we
love and with our God, and that will be heaven.

A Bible Reading:

Who shall separate us from the love of Christ?
Shall trouble or hardship or persecution or
famine or nakedness or danger or sword? As
it is written: 'For your sake we face death
all day long; we are considered as sheep to
be slaughtered.' No, in all these things, we
are more than conquerors through him who
loved us. For I am convinced that neither death
nor life, neither angels nor demons, neither
the present nor the future, nor any powers,
neither height nor depth, nor anything else in
all creation, will be able to separate us from the
love of God that is in Christ Jesus our Lord.

(Romans 8:35–39)

A Prayer

God of hope and the giver of all comfort, we pray for all who have been bereaved, and are beginning to build their lives again. Give us your peace within, your wisdom for each decision, your guidance for the direction we should take, and cause us to know that neither death nor life nor anything else can separate us from your love for us in Jesus Christ our Lord. Amen.

A Prayer

Notes

Chapter 1

[1] *Forte*, Autobiography of Charles Forte, Sidgwick, London, 1986, p 228.

[2] David M Owen, *Losing and Living*, Triangle, London, 1991, p 22.

[3] Beth Combe Harris, *This Earthly House*, no other details available.

Chapter 2

[1] A letter in *The Times*, dated 12 September 1959 by Robert Platt, quoted by Norman Autton, 'The Pastoral Care of the Dying', S.P.C.K., London, 1969, p 43.

[2] Luci Shaw, *God in the Dark*, Highland Books, Crowborough, 1990, p 19.

[3] Quoted from *Death in the First Person*, Anonymous, Copyright Feb.1970, The American Journal of Nursing Company.

[4] Norman Autton, *The Pastoral Care of the Dying*, S.P.C.K., London 1969 p 59.

[5] Adapted from Colquhoun, *'Contemporary Parish Prayers'* (number 454) Hodder & Stoughton, 1975, London, p 164.

Chapter 3
[1] C.S. Lewis, *The Problem of Pain*, Geoffrey Bles, London 1943 p 81.
[2] After J H Newman, quoted by Colquhoun in, 'Parish Prayers'. Edited Hodder & Stoughton, London 1967. Prayer 862.

Chapter 4
[1] Norman Autton, op cit, p 24.
[2] Adapted from Colquhoun, op cit, p 232.

Chapter 5
[1] Luci Shaw, op cit, p 169.
[2] Ibid page 172.
[3] Ibid page 179.
[4] Selwyn Hughes, *Everyday with Jesus*, Bible Reading notes from the Crusade for World Revival, 10 December 1990.
[5] Adapted from Colquhoun, op cit, p 156.

Chapter 6
[1] Quoted by Luci Shaw, op cit.
[2] Dr. Ruth Fowke, *Coping with Crisis*, Hodder & Stoughton, London 1968. pp 106–107.

Chapter 7
[1] John Carey, *The Daily Telegraph* for 5 May 1992.

Chapter 8

1 Frank Morrison, *Who Moved the Stone?* Faber & Faber, London, 1930.

2 Peter Marshall, *The First Easter*, Hodder & Stoughton, London, 1959, p 8.

3 Peter Marshall. ibid p 9–10.

4 *The Alternative Service Book*, Funeral Service 1980, Clowes, S P C K Cambridge University Press p 308.

Chapter 9

1 Canon Henry Scott Holland, Canon of St. Paul's Cathedral 1884–1911, quoted in Wendy Green, *Somebody I Love Has Died*, Lion, Oxford, 1990, p 28.

Chapter 10

1 Jeanne Scheresky 'Promise of Springtime', quoted in Wendy Green, op cit, p 36.

2 Wendy Green, ibid, p 8.

3 Tony Campolo, *Who Switched the Price Tags?*, Word Books, London 1986. p 28–29.

4 C.S. Lewis, *A Grief Observed*, Faber & Faber, London 1961 p 41.

5 Luci Shaw, op cit, pp 175 and 220.

Some organisations that may help

Cruse, 126 Sheen Road, Richmond, Surrey TW9 1UR (081–940 4818) will be able to give you the name and address of your local branch. (Cruse is a counselling service for the bereaved)

The Compassionate Friends, an organisation for bereaved parents. There are many local branches. The National Secretary can be contacted at: 50 Woodwaye, Watford, Herts WD1 4NW.

Some books that you might like to read

A Death in the Family by Jean Richardson, published by Lion

What happens after Death? by David Winter, published by Lion

Everlasting Spring by Philip Williams, published by Falcon.

Somebody I love has died, by Elaine Brown and Wendy Green, published by Lion.